TOPICS IN APPLIED GEOGRAPHY

SHOPPING CENTRE DEVELOPMENT

John A Dawson

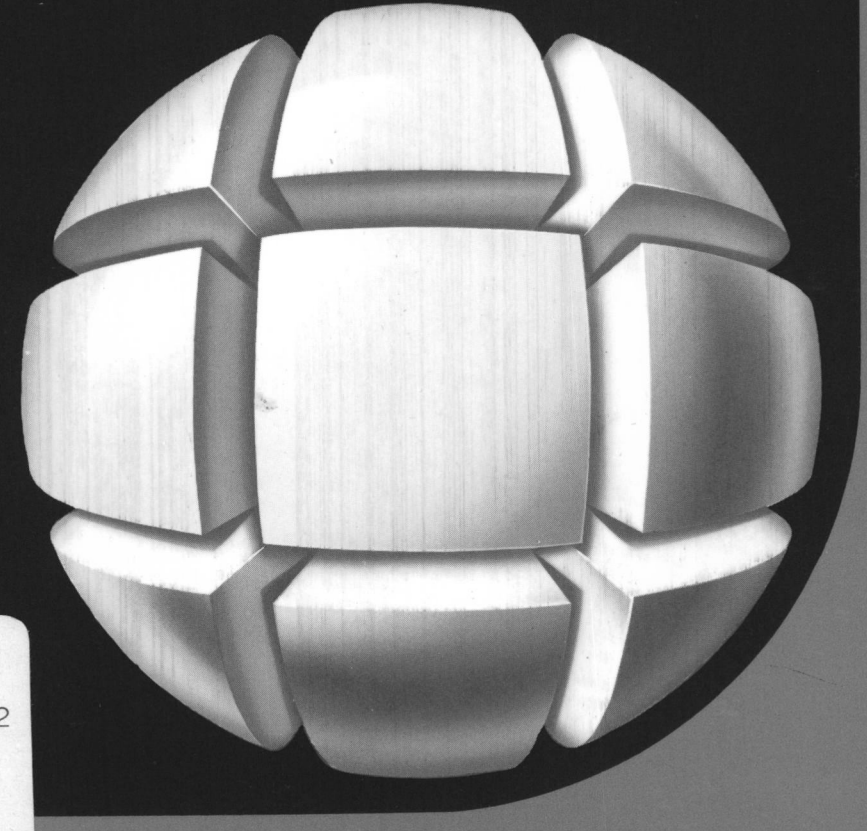

TOPICS IN APPLIED GEOGRAPHY

SHOPPING CENTRE DEVELOPMENT

TOPICS IN APPLIED GEOGRAPHY
edited by Donald Davidson and John Dawson

John A. Dawson
Saint David's University College
Lampeter

SHOPPING CENTRE DEVELOPMENT

Longman
London
and New York

Longman Group Limited
Longman House, Burnt Mill, Harlow
Essex CM20 2JE, England
Associated companies throughout the world

*Published in the United States of America
by Longman Inc., New York*

© J.A. Dawson 1983

First published 1983

British Library Cataloguing in Publication Data
Dawson, John
  Shopping centre development. – (Topics in applied geography)
  1. Shopping centres
  I. Title   II. Series
  711′.5522   HF5430

  ISBN 0-582-30068-1

Library of Congress Cataloging in Publication Data
Dawson, John A.
  Shopping centre development.

  (Topics in applied geography)
  Bibliography: p.
  Includes index.
  1. Shopping centers.   I. Title.   II. Series.
  HF5430.D38 1983   711′.5522   82-12674
  ISBN 0-582-30068-1

Printed in Singapore by
Selector Printing Co Pte Ltd.

Contents

LIST OF FIGURES

LIST OF TABLES

ACKNOWLEDGEMENTS

This book has been written in the hope that it will help geographers, and perhaps other social scientists, to understand a little more about one feature, but a particularly dynamic one, of the city. Thanks are due to many people who have helped me in the preparation of this book. The planners, developers, retailers and centre managers are too numerous to mention individually but thanks are due to them all for the hours they have spent with me. I should like to record my particular thanks to Donald Davidson for the gentleness of his editorial prompting, to colleagues, both staff and students, at Lampeter who have been a sounding board for the material in the book and to the staff of Longman for their enviable and unassuming professionalism in the total production process. Insights into shopping centre development were gained on two extended visits to Australia and I owe a considerable debt to Martyn Webb and Max Neutze, who made these visits possible and profitable, and to Ian Alexander, who encouraged me to try to understand Australian society. Grateful acknowledgement is made to the Nuffield Foundation, the International Communication Agency and the Pantyfedwyn Fund of St David's University College for grants towards fieldwork visits. Maureen Hunwicks typed the text impeccably and Trevor Harris was the more than adequate cartographer. To both I extend thanks for their effort and advice. Writing a book is as much a family task as it is the work of an individual and without Jo, Katherine and William this book would not have been what it is and so particular thanks to the latter two who have spent many hours in centres, have seldom complained and have become shopping centre children. To them this book is dedicated.

John Dawson
Lampeter
March, 1982

We are indebted to the following for permission to reproduce copyright material:

Professor Y. S. Cohen for Fig 4.1 (Cohen 1972); Pergamon Press Ltd for Table 6.3 (Bennison & Davies 1980) and Urban Land Institute for Fig 3.3 (Urban Land Institute 1980).

CHAPTER 1
THE GROWTH AND SPREAD OF SHOPPING CENTRES

Born in Europe, matured in North America, the shopping centre now exists in cities of widely different cultures and politics. Centres have become a feature of twentieth-century megaculture and as such they are a prominent element in modern urban landscapes as diverse as Houston and Hemel Hempstead or Bangkok and Budapest. The shopping centre as a part of the urban landscape is not new. Its history is as long as that of planned urban property developments, and in focusing attention on the shopping centre industry in the last thirty years most studies ignore the important nineteenth-century and earlier precursors of the modern shopping centre. In European cities many of these old centres remain as integral parts of modern shopping districts but attention tends to be focused on centres developed and built since 1945 or even since 1960.

DEFINITION

The term 'shopping centre' frequently is used rather loosely, simply to signify a group of shops. In the stricter sense used in this book, a shopping centre is defined as:

> A group of architecturally unified commercial establishments built on a site which is planned, developed, owned, and managed as an operating unit related in its location, size, and type of shops to the trade area that the unit serves (Urban Land Institute, 1977, p. 1). The unit usually provides on-site or associated car parking in definite relationship to the types and total size of the stores.

Although this definition was designed to isolate the essence of the modern American centre, it serves well as a general definition of a shopping centre. Its first value is that, by implication, it distinguishes the shopping centre from the shopping district. Shopping districts are simply concentrations of individual shops on individual sites providing some sort of general node for shopping activity. The shopping centre, in distinction, is a planned assemblage of shop units which may or may not exist as part of a shopping district. In most modern residential estates in Europe and North America a shopping centre has been designed, developed and built to provide shops for local residents. As such the shopping centre is free-standing. Alternatively in many British towns a section of the central area has been redeveloped as a shopping centre, which is effectively part of the central area shopping district. These redeveloped centres are often quite large, such as the 72 500 m^2 Eldon Square Centre in Newcastle-upon Tyne, but in many central area shopping districts there are also small centres perhaps of only ten or so shops which have been developed by private landlords and are integral parts of shopping districts. Whilst central area redevelopment shopping centres date mainly from the mid-1950s, these smaller centres within the fabric of the shopping district may be 100 years old and in some cases date from the urban commercial growth in Britain associated with the expansion of the railways.

In all periods of urban growth or major redevelopment since the nineteenth century shopping centres have been built. The massive suburban expansion in the USA in the last thirty years has produced the features of the urban landscape usually associated with the term 'shopping centre', but the British residential sprawl of the inter-war years, and earlier of the railway age, also generated shopping centres as did attempts to redevelop post-war urban Europe and nineteenth-century Paris. Shopping centres are a feature of the urban land development process in which landowners, both private and public, develop land deliberately for retail uses. This is the core idea in the definition provided above.

The unified architecture of the shopping centre usually makes it an obvious feature of the urban landscape. As the concept of the shopping centre has evolved over the past 100 years from being simply a terrace of shops to that of the carefully managed and promoted centres we see today, so architectural forms have changed to reflect the increasingly sophisticated image sought by the centre developers. As architecture has changed so also has function: improved management methods can make the shopping centre a positive and aggressive generator of consumer activity compared with the much more passive marketing concept of 100 years ago. Location, size and type of shop are carefully controlled in modern centres to maximize retail sales for the tenants. Architecture and function come together in the new centres where completely artificial shopping environments are created in massive enclosed structures. The shopping environment in such centres is totally controlled, initially through a complicated design and development process and subsequently through an equally sophisticated management operation. Whilst the shopping centre always has been designed in relation to its trade area, with increasingly aggressive marketing this relationship has become symbiotic with centre and trade area being inter-related rather than the centre being dependent on the trade area. With changing consumption patterns and consumer behaviour processes, trade area analyses are increasingly concerned with consumer segments rather than with the total consumer group and shopping centres have played a part in promoting the fragmentation of consumer patterns and in serving the various segments. Speciality shopping centres, for example, are now being developed which consist of shops selling only one group of goods such as craft articles or ladies' high fashion. By controlling and managing the mix of tenants, a centre can be managed as a unit to the economic benefit of both developers and tenants. Out of this development and management process, the shopping centre industry has emerged as a multi-million-pound sector of western economies.

THE EVOLUTION OF THE SHOPPING CENTRE IDEA

From its origins in eighteenth- and nineteenth-century arcades and shop terraces the shopping centre development industry has changed from being the business of small landlords to an activity whose market leaders are multinational development enterprises owning centres in many cities and in different countires. Much of the growth has occurred since 1940 as development and management methods have become able to cope with large-scale investments and massive shopping structures. There has also been a massive increase in recent decades in the number of small centres of around ten or twelve shop units. The lucrative financial opportunities presented to property developers and land speculators has been a major feature in the widespread investment in shopping centres and the emergence of a shopping centre industry. Urban growth and urban redevelopment have provided opportunities which, particularly in North America, have been grasped both by established property companies and by many new entrants to the field. The success of the shopping centre industry in providing retail sites is such that in the USA over 40 per cent of retail sales pass through large shopping centres. When small, strip or terrace developments are included in the definition of shopping centres, then this proportion rises to well over 50 per cent. In Britain the proportion is much less and estimates vary, depending on the precise definition of centres, with between 15 per cent and 25 per cent of retail sales being accounted for by shopping centres. In both the USA and in Britain sales through shopping centres are growing at a faster rate than retail sales generally, resulting in a steadily increasing proportion of trade accountable to these centres.

The evolution of the concept of the shopping centre and also of the size and importance of the development industry have been rapid in the post-war years and much of this book is concerned with this period of change. There were some significant developments before 1940, however, and the success of these clearly helped in the political, social and economic acceptance of shopping centres in later years.

In Britain, Burns (1959) has described the change in suburban shop provision which accompanied the intense housing building activity of the 1920s and 1930s. Writing of this period he states,

> Isolated and scattered shops were now frowned upon . . . It now became the pattern to group shops into small centres of four or six or even ten shops and to plan these centres to serve as conveniently as possible all residents on the estate. Little regard was paid to what was happening on an adjoining estate, but since each developer tried to make his own estate self-sufficient there was not much conflict (p. 7).

These proto-neighbourhood centres provided shops for professional shopkeepers, unlike many previous single shop buildings where the shop was part of the residence and was used as a means of supplementing family income; they also provided larger units creating a potential for the subsequent acceptance of the new retail technologies, such as self-service. Many hundreds of such centres were built and most still operate as small suburban shopping centres.

The reason for this rash of small suburban centres in Britain is complex. The growth of residential suburbia is clearly of paramount importance but the acceptance of the centre concept as a means of shop provision 'may have resulted from the new planning theories and orderly estate development which was undertaken by private enterprise. It may, on the other hand, have been simply a question of good estate management and a means of maximizing the profits from any given development' (Burns, p. 7). It was not only on private enterprise estates that this form of commercial development occurred, but also comparable small centres were built by local government on public housing estates. These centres are still plentiful in suburban Britain and are managed by local authority estates departments which control, albeit rather weakly in many cases, the mix of businesses operating in the centre.

The success of these centres resulted from the spatial monopoly their tenants held over the area of the estate coupled with the low mobility levels of consumers living on the estate. Convenience goods for households were purchased on daily walks to the shops with heavier purchases often being delivered by retailers in the centre. The commercial success of retail tenants, the resulting financial success for developers, the consumer satisfaction of being able to make multi-purpose shopping trips to a place of relatively intense social activity, were all factors that encouraged land use planners in the post-war period to plan positively for neighbourhood centres in the British New Towns and in the planned post-war suburban residential expansion. The earlier developments in the 1920s and 1930s in Britain are nevertheless important precursors to the widespread acceptance and expansion of shopping centres in post-war urban Britain.

EARLY DEVELOPMENTS IN THE USA

Within the USA there were isolated experiments in shopping centre development in the nineteenth century and in the early years of this century but again important breakthroughs in design, development and operation date from the 1920s and 1930s. In 1827 Cyrus Butler built a fifty-shop, three-level enclosed shopping arcade in Providence, Rhode Island and opened it two years later (*Shopping Center World*, 1978a). In 1907 Edward H. Boulton built the Roland Park shopping centre in Baltimore as part of a high-status residential community. By the 1920s there had begun in some American cities the decentralization of general merchandise stores into free-standing shops at key intersections in the expanding suburban transport network. The emergence of supermarketing methods with their demands for more extensive sites also resulted in the building of free-standing stores in the suburbs. 'Under developer enterprise these experiments were soon scaled to a unified row of stores with display windows fronting on traffic streets and on-lot parking for customers at the rear or side of the strip' (Urban Land Institute, 1977, p. 12). By the late 1920s these *strip centres* were becoming commonplace in commercially buoyant suburban America from New York to Los Angeles.

The growth of such centres in Chicago has been described by Hoyt (1933), and Proudfoot (1937) and his co-worker (Mayer, 1942). Applebaum (1932) and his collaborator (Applebaum and Schapker, 1956) considered the phenomenon in Cincinnati. Sabit and Black (1962) analysed growth in Detroit; in Los Angeles the study by Cassady and Bowden (1944) measured the extent of retail decentralization from 1929 to 1939, with the implication being that much suburban development was occurring in strip centres and in the 1930s in larger centres such as the Santa Barbara-Crenshaw centre. Development in Chicago owed much to the acumen of Robert Wood, the Vice-President of Sears Roebuck (Emmet and Jeuck, 1950). This company, founded in 1886, became a major mail-order company by 1900, supplying the rural population from a Chicago base. With the Montgomery Ward Company, Sears Roebuck dominated mail order until 1919 when sales levelled off and then collapsed following the sharp decline in commodity prices and the drop in rural income in 1921–22. Robert Wood's reaction was to diversify the business and establish general merchandise stores at key public transport intersections in Chicago's rapidly expanding suburbs. From providing for a conservative rural consumer through mail order, company policy changed to that of providing for urban consumers through fixed stores. These Sears Roebuck suburban stores provided the nucleus for many strip centres. The first store opened in 1926 and there were 192 by 1928, notably in Chicago. The policy and development pattern begun in the mid-1920s continued for several decades. Some of the new stores served as the nucleus for new shopping districts, not just for small shopping centres, and Hoyt (1933) pointed to the emergence by 1929 of 16 leading suburban shopping districts comprising small shopping centres but with considerable additional general retail development. By 1933 Proudfoot isolated 33 such districts and over 50 minor suburban shopping districts, the majority of which contained a strip centre within them. The emergence of strip centres as a viable form of environment for retail operation and as a form of property investment, as shown by their rapid increase in land value, was one of two important features of the early shopping centre industry in the USA.

The second feature involved the creation of larger shopping developments providing shop units for comparison and for fashion retailers as well for retailers of convenience goods. These may be seen as extensions of the idea of a strip centre, not only in the way their form and structure developed, but also in the personal associations between the developers and designers of the early centres. Boulton, the developer of Roland Park, had a strong influence through personal meetings and discussions, on J. C. Nichols and H. Potter who were respectively responsible for developing the Country Club Plaza in Kansas City in 1922–23, and the River Oaks Centre in Houston in 1937. All three were important in forming, in 1936, the Urban Land Institute, which has been a powerful force in diffusing new ideas on shopping centre design and operation.

The Country Club Plaza today has 280 tenants. The shopping centre is a series of individual blocks of shop units in a coordinated development with unified architectural style, landscaping, management policy, sign control and so on. The River Oaks Centre, Houston was developed, as was the County Club Plaza, to serve a high-status residential development. In both cases public roads crossed the centres. Figure 1.1 shows the layout of River Oaks as it is today with its 47 stores and 32 500 m² of leaseable space. The original buildings of the late 1930s and 1940s are alongside a central spine road with a 1972 extension at the eastern end of the centre. A third example of these larger centres which were developed in the USA in the 1930s is the Highland Park Centre in Dallas. In common with others in Boston, Baltimore, Cleveland and Ardmore, Philadelphia, these larger centres were built in high-status, high-income areas with a generally upmarket tenant mix. The high-status residential areas have tended to be stable and the centres remain dominated by comparison fashion retailers. The Dallas centre was developed in 1931 by H. Potter; he also knew of the

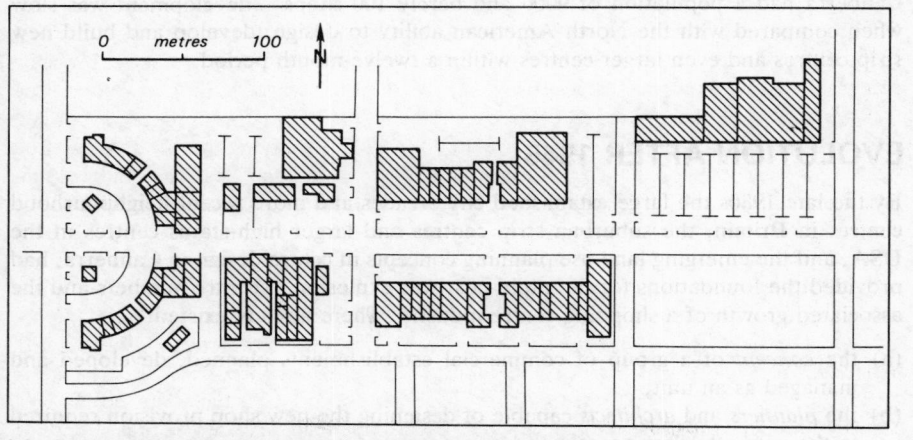

1.1 Layout of the River Oaks Shopping Centre, Houston, Texas

Roland Park scheme and he pioneered the style of turning the shop frontages away from the street and providing off-street parking. This significant innovation leads the Urban Land Institute (1977) to suggest that Highland Park 'can accurately be called the prototype for the present-day planned shopping centre – the site all in one piece, not bisected by public streets, with individual stores built and managed as an unit with an unified image, under single ownership control and with the amount of on-site parking determined by parking demand' (p. 14).

EARLY SCHEMES IN AUSTRALIA

The Australian cities of the 1930s were also undergoing rapid growth and again some attempts were being made to develop shopping centres. The influences from Britain were strong but designs were tempered by American experience and by the Australian environment. The few centres developed in this period were small suburban strips of up to a dozen or so shops which were either part of a larger shopping district or formed the core for later piecemeal development of a shopping district. As in the British examples management was weak and, even more than in Britain, the motive for development was developer profit with local government playing virtually no significant role. There is one notable exception which had considerable implications for later shopping centre developments. The founding and gradual growth in the 1920s of Canberra within a firmly planned overall design which included shopping centre provision provided a working example to the nascent shopping centre industry (Linge, 1975). By the mid-1930s several small neighbourhood centres had been built to serve the growing suburban development but shop mix in such centres was atypical of developments in Britain and USA as the neighbourhood shops effectively were the only shops, there being no central area shops at this time. The development of a New City from a greenfield site meant that the only shops were in shopping centres and in the early years relatively few were provided. The emerging planned city centre had similarities, architecturally, with the larger suburban centres similarly developed in the early 1930s in the USA but functionally it was quite different. It was nonetheless a unified, planned and managed commercial area and laid the foundations for the later development of centres in the city. It must be remembered that in the mid-1930s Canberra had a population of 9000 and barely 100 shops – development was slow when compared with the North American ability to design, develop and build new strip centres and even larger centres within a twelve-month period.

EVOLUTION AFTER 1945

By the late 1930s the large established city arcades and more recent neighbourhood centres in Britain, the suburban strip centres and larger high-status centres in the USA, and the emerging land use planning concepts in centre design in Canberra, had provided the foundations for the rapid post-war explosion in centre numbers and the associated growth of a shopping centre industry. There already existed:

(a) the *concept* of a group of commercial establishments planned, developed and managed as an unit;
(b) the *planners* and *architects* capable of designing the new shop provision required in the new suburban areas;

(c) the *developers*, both private enterprise and government, providing the finance and organization for the building process;
(d) the *retailers* willing to trade in the new commercial environment created by shopping centres;
(e) the *consumers* embarking on the road to a mass consumption economy, becoming more mobile, increasingly suburban and willing to undertake and finance multipurpose shopping trips.

All that was needed in the post-war years were the two catalysts of urban growth and economic growth, the one to provide population concentrations, the other to provide consumers with spending power.

The catalysts were present in the USA before 1940, and though their power was lessened in the war years, by 1945 rapid development was underway. In Europe economic growth was slower in reaching the critical point to sustain mass consumption by the population and large centres did not blossom until the 1960s. In Australia the position was an intermediate one but in Eastern Europe and in many Asian, African and Latin American countries the self-sustaining process of shopping centre development did not begin until the 1970s. In the poorer Third World countries, although urban growth has been rapid in recent years, the inherent poverty of the consumers currently militates against the widespread development of large shopping centres to serve indigenous populations. In the years since 1940, however, the shopping centre has become a megacultural feature of the urban landscape. Whilst the basic idea is widely accepted, several distinct evolutionary strands have emerged from the proto-centres of the 1930s. The resulting typology of centres is considered in the next chapter but it is worthwhile considering briefly here the diffusion of the centre concept to its present world-wide distribution.

The spread of the shopping centre idea and its translation into an urban landscape feature in the USA was rapid in the post-war phase of suburban expansion. Initially in this period centres were located in established and growing suburban districts essentially following the spatial spread of residences. Suburban spread in the north-eastern cities and in California provided near optimal locations for shopping centre investment and centres were built by both the developers originally involved in strip centres and by several new entrants to the shopping centre industry who have, in barely twenty-five years, subsequently become very large companies. In 1928 the first centre designed by Don M. Casto Sr. opened in Columbus, Ohio, and was followed by other strip centres (Thil, 1966). By 1948 the same company was developing and planning a chain of Town and Country Shopping Centres throughout suburban Columbus and later moved on to other cities. The first Town and Country centre is on a site 10 km east of the Columbus CBD which in 1948 was the edge of the built-up area. The centre was built with an investment of $50 000 by Casto and $450 000 by the Phoenix Insurance Company. There were 10 000 families in the immediate suburban surroundings but the success of the centre, through its ease of shopping, ample free parking and policy of staying open until 9 p.m., was such that it was attracting shoppers from 30 km away. This success led to rapid repayment of loan finance and made a massive profit for the developer. In the period 1951–56 Casto built a new centre each year in suburban Columbus and by 1966 had developed 8 of the 27 centres then operating in the city. The centres each had between 40 and 100 shops comprising 15 000 to 50 000 m^2 sales area on sites of between 20 to 40 ha. The rapidity of expansion not only of the Casto Company but also of the spread of shopping centres in Columbus is typical of the growth of developers and of the spread of centres. In the

Table 1.1 Leading American shopping centre developers in January, 1981

DEVELOPER	HOME STATE	GLA DEVELOPED	GLA OWNED	NUMBER OF CENTRES OWNED OVER 100 000 m²
Taubman	Michigan	6.04	2.74	15
Edward J. De Bartolo	Ohio	5.16	4.80	21
Homart Development	Illinois	3.82	1.50	4
Melvin Simon and Associates	Indiana	3.17	2.92	9
Ernest W. Hahn	California	3.04	2.05	6
Rouse	Maryland	2.51	2.51	6
Strouse, Greenberg	Pennsylvania	2.27	1.10	0
Cafaro	Ohio	2.05	1.91	2
Jacobs/Kahan Jacobs, Visconti and Jacobs	Illinois	2.00	1.51	3
	Ohio	1.71	1.68.	6
Kravco	Pennsylvania	1.51	1.54	8
Crown American	Pennsylvania	1.50	1.43	0

early post-war period the centre concept was advocated strongly by some key architects, such as Victor Guen, who were important in providing the technical expertise for the emerging developer organization. Table 1.1 lists the largest developers in the USA in 1981; the Casto organization is in thirty-sixth place with 758 000 m² of developed floorspace (*Gross Leasable Area* (GLA): see definition in the Appendix) in January 1981. The company still owns all the centres it has developed. The top ranking developer, the Taubman Company, dates from the post-war boom period and in thirty years of existence has developed a massive 6 million m² of development but has sold over half the space it has developed having ownership, in 1981, of 2.7 million m² of space. This is considerably less than the area owned by the largest company, the Edward J. De Bartolo Corporation, which also dates from the early post-war years. Centres were developed in the 1950s on the edge of the suburbs only to become engulfed in the spread of suburbia so allowing new centres to be built again on the urban fringe. This pattern was typical of cities throughout the industrial north-east USA and in California in the 1950s and early 1960s. In an analysis limited to large suburban centres Cohen (1972) has shown a diffusion westward and southward from the industrial north-east: 'from 1955 to 1958 and from 1959 to 1963, the spread can been seen "advancing" west and south' (p. 39). This spatial spread is tempered by a hierarchial diffusion pattern in which 'It is specifically evident that within states the largest or second largest cities adopted the innovation before other cities' (p. 39). With recent changes in patterns of population growth the main developments have shifted to the southern states and the sunbelt cities but the development industry has lost little in impetus despite changes in governments, oil crises and world recessions (see Ch. 4). In 1980, 336 000 m² GLA of new shopping centres were built in Dallas and this was a 40 per cent drop on the 1979 figure. In many major northern cities development levels are less than 10 per cent of this Dallas rate. The shift to the sunbelt is a major trend apparent in shopping centre development in the USA but much of the development expertise still comes from the major companies based in north-eastern cities (see Table 1.1). By 1981 over 20 000 shopping centres of over 1000 m² were operating in the USA.

The dominance of private enterprise developers in this surge of development and construction activity in the USA shopping centre industry has meant that centres have been located in the potentially most profitable locations. These are suburban middle- and higher-income districts. Relatively few centres, and this is particularly true of the large centres, have been located in the low-income inner suburbs or in ghetto areas, whether black ghettos of northern cities or the Mexican ghettos of Texan cities. The contrast with Britain and the diffusion of centres through Britain since 1945 is particularly strong in this respect. The Town and Country Planning Act of 1947 meant that local government agencies were involved, to some degree, in all shopping centre developments since that date and in many cases were able to act as catalysts for the development of centres. Suburban population growth was contained to a considerable extent by the policies of selected town expansion and New Town building. The building of new shopping centres in the 1940s and 1950s in Britain was therefore a continuation of the pre-war trends of neighbourhood centre building, and importantly also arose from the creation of new town centres on greenfield sites in New Towns and from the redevelopment of small or war-damaged centres in expanding towns. It was the success of these various schemes that led to the large number of central city redevelopment shopping centres planned and opened since the late 1950s.

POST-WAR TRENDS IN BRITAIN

In an analysis of city centre redevelopment shopping developments, Davies and Bennison (1979) argue that 'In many ways the precinct developments established after the Second World War in such heavily bombed cities as Coventry, Plymouth and Southampton, constitute a first stage in a general evolutionary process whereby new shopping facilities have become increasingly more compact and physically separate from other land uses'. This is essentially the shopping centre concept. 'A second stage can be recognised in the formation of new town centres for the New Towns although these were often built on greenfield sites and hence may be more appropriately linked to the history of suburban development.' These schemes, however, provided the land use planner and architect with experience in shopping centre development. 'The third stage is more clear cut, being marked by the building of the first enclosed centres and the integration of these into comprehensive redevelopment programmes for the central city' (p. 192). This third stage marks the entry, in a significant way, of the property developer into the growing shopping centre industry.

> The third stage really began in 1964 with the opening of the Bull Ring Centre in Birmingham. This was shortly followed by the Elephant and Castle scheme in London (1965), the Marian centre in Leeds (1965) and the first of the town centre Arndale schemes in Doncaster in 1968 . . . All were largely products of Development Plans produced (by local land use planning authorities) in the middle and late 1950s, the forerunners of a subsequent decade of plans preoccupied with town centre revitalization and environmental improvement (p. 192).

This local government emphasis on new shopping schemes was encouraged by central government policies and advice on town centre renewal. Three *Planning Bulletins* produced by the Ministry of Housing and Local Government in 1962 and 1963 provided advice, pointed to the need to renew town centres and stressed the importance of involving private enterprise in the commercial aspects of shopping centre development. The ministerial foreword to *Bulletin 1* states that 'Town centre redevelopment is essentially a matter for co-operation between local government and private enterprise . . . Private initiative must be harnessed to planned redevelopment, not allowed to dictate it' (p. 1). The *Bulletin* later points out, 'the normal agency for carrying out the subsequent commercial development is private enterprise. Private developers have the capital and expertise and they are generally willing to take the risk inherent in new development provided that the terms are reasonable' (p. 7). The partnership between government and private enterprise is central to understanding the way shopping centres have spread throughout urban Britain. The formal land use control mechanisms operated by government have provided the framework, both spatial and structural, in which the development process and the shopping centre industry has operated.

As in the USA, major development companies have emerged in the last twenty years and two companies stand apart from the rest. Table 1.2 lists the ten largest companies which together account for 51 per cent of developed floor space in centres over 4645 m². In some cases in Britain a local government authority has acted as a developer for a centre in its own district. One result of the involvement of local government in shopping centre development generally has been the building of centres in response to the needs for a centre rather than as a response to an opportunity to make a profit in the development process. Thus there is in Britain, in contrast to the USA, a relatively even spread of centre development without emphasis on developing first in middle- and higher-income areas. A more equitable pattern of access to centres is apparent in Britain as a result. The London region, however, was rather late in having shopping centres because of land use planning agency decisions, not because of the developers. Schiller and Lambert (1977) have shown that in 1976 in London only 10 of the 29 large shopping districts had central area shopping centres in operation compared with 37 out of the 46 largest central areas in the relatively less prosperous north of England (see Ch. 4). Since the mid-1970s this relative deprivation of London has lessened and shopping centres, even if only small ones, are now operational or planned for almost all the major shopping districts in London.

Table 1.2 Leading British shopping centre developers in January, 1981

DEVELOPER	HQ CITY	GLA DEVELOPED (MILLION M²)	NUMBER OF SCHEMES DEVELOPED
Town and City	London	0.767	38
Ravenseft	London	0.568	39
Hammerson	London	0.364	16
Laing	Watford	0.221	15
EPC	London	0.185	21
Grosvenor	London	0.170	7
Capital and Countries	London	0.152	4
Norwich Union	Norwich	0.145	10
CIN	London	0.099	4
Neale House	London	0.095	5
Local authorities combined		0.378	23
New Town Development Corporations		0.374	21

Note: The data refer only to shopping centres of 4645 m² and larger
Source: Hillier Parker May and Rowden (1981)

Although the cynosure of planners and developers in Britain has been the central area redevelopment shopping centres, a range of other types of centre have been created. The extent of the growth of shopping centres in Britain has not been charted but estimates suggest that 30 000 m² of neighbourhood and strip shopping centre space has been constructed in the last fifty years and that by 1981 there were probably close to 1000 shopping centres of other types in operation.

CENTRE DEVELOPMENT ELSEWHERE IN EUROPE

A variety of types of centre is also seen in other Western European countries and Scandinavia. The rapid growth in centre numbers has occurred since 1965 in most of these countries. In France again there is quite a long history of small centres but for medium and large centres the major period of growth has been since the late 1960s as is shown in Figure 1.2 (Dawson, 1981). The growth in numbers was accompanied, as might be expected, with a spatial spread of centres through the urban system. Although the timing differs from country to country the various preconditions for centre development have all been met in urban Europe and by the early 1980s the shopping centre had become an established feature of townscapes and of society itself. Perhaps with the spread of centres throughout the city the shopping centre is more generally accessible to all sections of the population in Britain, France or Sweden than it is in the USA.

Alongside the post-war reconstruction and New Town planning in Britain some of the most influential early centres were those developed in Sweden. During the 1950s several New Town schemes were planned within new suburban communities which had shopping centres associated with other social land uses located strategically within the city transport network (Strong, 1971; Westerman, 1966; Scarlat, 1963; Pass, 1973). New housing districts were planned and built often with 5000–10 000 residents and within the housing areas shopping centres were built. The new communities resulting from the planned decentralization of Stockholm provide some early European examples of multi-use shopping centres. The centre at Färsta, for example, which was opened in 1954, was developed by private enterprise with government encouragement to provide a focus for the suburban community of 25 000 people south of Stockholm. In the same year the much larger centre at Vällingby was opened providing 9700 m² of retail sales space which soon proved inadequate and which was doubled by building on car park areas and providing multi-storey car parks. The centre is not simply a shopping centre; it contains approximately equal amounts of retail and office/services space. The Stockholm planning authorities oversaw the creation of these shopping centres in the planned suburban communities and imposed a strict four-tier hierarchy of shopping centres with each hierarchy being distinct in size and range of functions. Plans were drawn up for:

(a) local centres serving 4000–7000 people;
(b) neighbourhood centres serving 15 000 people;
(c) district centres serving 120 000 people;
(d) regional centres serving 500 000 people.

In 1981 there were over a hundred centres in existence in the Stockholm region although not all were in the newer suburban residential areas. Other cities in Sweden followed the example provided in Stockholm and again by the mid-1960s most cities had and were planning major shopping centre schemes either to renew town centres

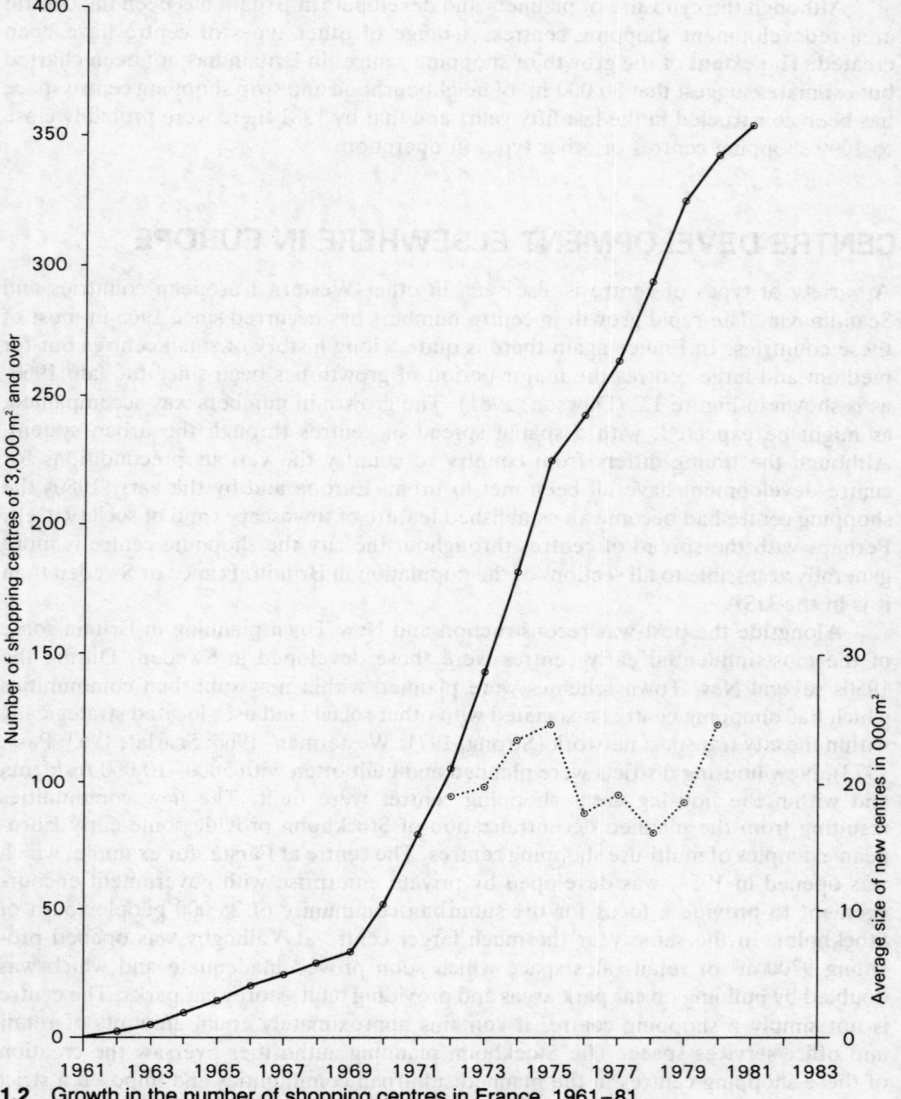

1.2 Growth in the number of shopping centres in France, 1961–81.

or to provide new centres in the suburbs. As in Britain, government played an active role in centre development and in Sweden there was emphasis on encouraging private sector participation. Although most schemes are commercially successful in development terms, the purpose of centre provision was not to make a profit but to provide a high level of accessibility to retail and other services.

Whilst the role of the social planner is almost absent in the centre development process in the USA, in Sweden social planning is an important factor and in Eastern Europe, the USSR and Israel, the social planner is the determining influence on the form and function of shopping centres as well as on the development process. The presence of shopping centres in such contrasting political and social environments points to them being a megacultural aspect of urbanism.

Within the socialist cities of Eastern Europe and the USSR, shopping centres have yet to be built in large numbers. A change in socialist planning philosophy coupled with greater expectations from the consumer resulted in plans and developments during the late 1970s in several large socialist cities. The five preconditions to centre development listed above together with the two catalysts of urban growth and increased consumer spending power are now present and shopping centres are being built and proving successful within socialist economic systems.

In the USSR and Eastern Europe until the early 1970s, shopping facilities showed little concentration other than in the shopping districts which had developed in pre-socialist days. Retail provision in the new residential areas tended to be scattered on the ground floor of blocks of flats or were dispersed in single shop units through the housing area. Not only is there consumer inconvenience in such a pattern but also it leads to a highly inefficient pattern of physical distribution of goods to the shops. Discussing Moscow, French (1979) suggests that 'Recently this lack of convenience has evoked calls for the establishment of local shopping precincts, distributed rationally through the urban area so that no-one is more than ten minutes walk away' (p. 95). In East European countries city land use planners and Ministry of Domestic Trade retail planners are moving away from ideas of dispersed provision to plans providing concentrations of retailing in purpose-built shopping centres. The Hungarian planners, for example, incorporate small centres of up to 10 000 m² in large new housing areas, such as those around Debrecen and other key cities, whilst the city plan for Budapest includes the creation of several centres at key transport intersections in the middle suburbs (Perenyi, 1973). Development of these centres in the case of Budapest is a partnership between central government, city government and large retail trade enterprises. The active involvement of the retailers is interesting and reminiscent of the early developments in pre-war USA.

THE SPREAD OF CENTRES WORLD-WIDE

With the shopping centre development in the newly settled lands in Israel the bases of comparison lie with the British and Swedish New Town schemes. With new settlement planning on greenfield sites a hierarchy of shopping centres of different sizes has been incorporated into the master plans of these settlements (Strong, 1971; Spiegel, 1966). With such communities the development process for shopping centres can be extremely rapid if population build-up is similarly rapid, but the process may be very slow when on the one hand the population is unwilling to move until a centre has been built and on the other hand the developers are unwilling to commit themselves to a centre until the population has reached a critical level. In settlements such as Ashdod and Beer Sheva, strong centres in the residential neighbourhoods come before major centres acting as a focus for the whole community. Shopping centre development is, however, an established major plank in New Town development whether in Israel, Britain, Holland, Sweden or Finland and is becoming an increasingly accepted feature of such planning schemes in socialist economies.

The shopping centres in New Towns and new suburbs aim to provide facilities accessible to the mass of population. The shopping centre development in the Third World has moved in two directions – one toward mass consumer provision and the other aimed at a highly segmented consumer market. The first type usually has a strong government presence in the development process and is typified by the centres provided in the new housing areas in Singapore, Hong Kong and Kuala Lumpur (Yeung and Yeh, 1971; Abdullah, 1971). Small centre provision, with ten to fifteen shops providing a range of convenience goods, is a common feature of development plans in Third World cities even in the poorest countries, as Bijlani's (1977) review of development planning in Gangtok in Sikkim shows. The plan 'proposes 4 new Neighbourhood Centres are developed in the proposed residential areas. Each Neigh-bourhood Centre would have approximately one hectare area and would provide for 15 to 20 large and medium sized shops with a number of small shops for fruit and vegetable sellers . . .' The plan also incorporates proposals 'to locate local shopping centres comprising 6 to 8 small shops in the new residential areas and the areas pro-posed to be redeveloped'(p. 99). Such an approach is typical of many cities in the Third World. The second type has a greater private-enterprise developer element and is typified by the shopping centres within hotel complexes in Bangkok, Manila or Hong Kong and also by developments aimed at the small number of wealthy middle class consumers in cities such as Lima, Nairobi or Mexico City. Within Third World countries shopping centre development is in its infancy but already there exist, built within the last ten years, a considerable variety of types of centres. Much has been learnt from the successes and mistakes of the shopping centre industry of the USA, Australia and Europe. Already some major development companies are emerging, such as the Ayola Corporation in Manila, which owns over 200 000 m² of shopping centre space. More generally the local development companies are smaller but there is increasing interest by American and European developers in the market potential apparent in the Third World cities. In the last twenty years there has been a growth in the numbers of transatlantic developers with investments and centres in both North America and Europe. Already there has been development activity by North Amer-ican companies in Latin America's cities with the Sears organization pioneering sev-eral schemes of 20 000 m² and over (Campbell, 1974). The next twenty years may well see increases in this activity by North American and European developers in the Third World.

The aim of the preceding pages has been to give an indication of the megacultural aspects of shopping centres in respect of the acceptance of the concept. Little or no mention has been made of contemporary shopping centre development in Australia, Canada, Japan, South Africa or Venezuela nor of many other countries where shop-ping centres have become, since the early 1960s, an established feature of city struc-ture. Whilst the details of the form and function of shopping centres is constantly evolving and bears a strong cultural imprint, the concept of a single architectural unit, developed and managed as an entity but composed of several retail units, is one that is now accepted in many diverse cultures as being an efficient and acceptable element of the modern city.

THE EMERGENCE OF THE SHOPPING CENTRE INDUSTRY

The essence of the shopping centre development process is the co-ordination of the expertise of several different organizations and professions. Figure 1.3 provides a gen-eral model of the relationships amongst the groups involved. The process as it operates in different countries can be represented by slight variations on this diagram. In some cases the developer and property consultant are one organization or the property con-

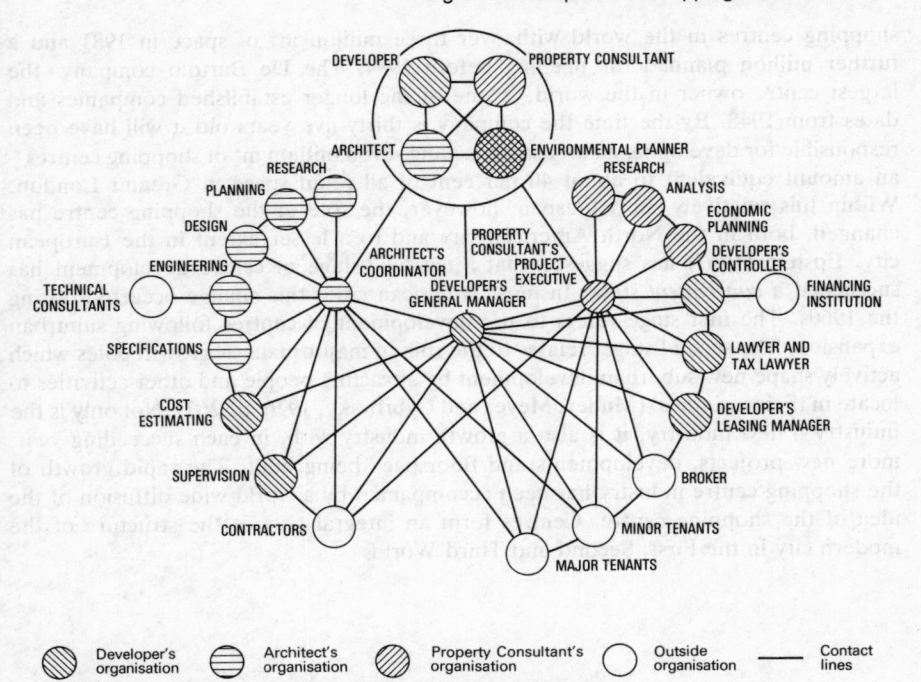

1.3 The participants in the shopping centre development process.

sultant may be effectively, as in Eastern Europe, a government agency working along with the developer. The core of the diagram and of the development process is the interaction of the four organizations of developer, architect, property consultant and environmental or land use planner. Specialist information is passed into each of these organizations and this specialist data comes from within each organization and from other groups outside the four organizations. There is scope for great variation in the extent of organizational overlap amongst the various activities and groups shown in Figure 1.3. In some cases development is highly integrated with a single large corporation acting as general developer, using its own funds, and developing the centre through its own architecture department and leasing to tenants which are part of the overall corporation. In other cases development is disintegrated amongst many different and independent organizations. The development process is considered in detail in Chapter 3.

Decisions on the location and type of centre result from the interactions amongst the four organizations at the core of this diagram. It is interesting that in this development process the consumer, who after all is the ultimate user of the centre, plays a relatively minor role. The land use planner is to some extent the custodian of the consumer interest and the developer's successes or failures ultimately rest on the consumer's willingness to use the shopping centre. Nevertheless the consumer, perhaps because of the lack of a formal consumer organization, is not directly involved in the development process.

The shopping centre industry is a new industry although its origins can be traced back to the nineteenth century. Industry growth since the mid-1950s has been rapid and twenty years is considered a long time within the industry. Melvin Simon and Associates, for example, was founded in 1960 and is now the second largest owner of shopping centres in the world with over three million m^2 of space in 1981 and a further million planned for opening before 1984. The De Bartolo company, the largest centre owner in the world, is one of the longer established companies and dates from 1948. By the time the company is thirty-five years old it will have been responsible for developing an area approaching seven million m^2 of shopping centres – an amount equivalent to about 40 per cent of all retail space in Greater London. Within this relatively short lifespan, however, the role of the shopping centre has changed, both in the North American city and to a lesser extent in the European city. Epstein (1967) has suggested that a *catalytic* stage of centre development has succeeded a *consequent* state. In most American cities this change occurred during the 1960s. The first stage refers to the development of centres following suburban expansion. The second stage 'relates to the role of major malls as growth poles which actively shape new suburban development by attracting people and other activities to locate in their vicinities' (Muller, Meyer and Cybriwsky, 1976, p. 267). Not only is the industry a new industry, it is also a growth industry with, in each succeeding year, more new projects, developments and floorspace being built. The rapid growth of the shopping centre industry has been accompanied by a world-wide diffusion of the idea of the shopping centre. Centres form an integral part of the structure of the modern city in the First, Second and Third Worlds.

CHAPTER 2
TYPES OF SHOPPING CENTRE

The rapid growth in numbers and the world-wide diffusion of shopping centres in the last thirty years are associated with a steady evolution of centre form. A number of clearly discernible shopping centre types have evolved in the post-war decades. Some types can be traced back directly to their 1920s ancestors, others have resulted from cross-breeding and the hybridization of centre types during their evolution. As an architectural and commercial entity within the city, the shopping centre continues to evolve and new forms appear. Such an anthropomorphic view of change in the shopping centre industry is commonly used to provide some order to the patterns' of change, but it must be remembered that the shape of the industry and the form and characteristics of centres result not from some process of natural selection but from conscious decisions made by the four core groups, shown in Figure 1.3, in the development process. Whilst it is possible to describe relationships and similarities amongst the different centre types, it is necessary to relate the types to their process of development in order to fully understand the reasons why different types occur. The aim of this chapter is to review the types of centre in operation and in Chapter 3 the development process will be considered in more detail.

Much of the impetus for shopping centre development came from the USA and by the mid-1950s three main types of shopping centre had been recognized by developers, architects, planners and geographers (Urban Land Institute, 1977; Bell, 1975; Gosling and Maitland, 1976; Jones, 1969; Baker and Funaro, 1951; Chapin, 1965; McGregor, 1960; Berry, 1959, 1967; Garner, 1966; Hoyt, 1958; Gruen and Smith, 1960; Welch, 1969). The three types are: *neighbourhood centre*; *community centre*; and *regional centre*. The acceptance of this three-fold classification has given it an enduring place in centre planning activities and has resulted in considerable ossification in attitudes to new types of centre. The three-tiered hierarchy has become one of the established truths of modern urban geography, yet it really describes the centre developments begun in the 1950s. This classification has remained in common use despite the subsequent development of many çentres which clearly do not fit any of the three categories. This classification remains applicable to the 'traditional' suburban centre concept and essentially it is based on the size of centre, together with related function and *tenant mix*.

THE NEIGHBOURHOOD CENTRE

The function of the *neighbourhood centre* is to provide a range of convenience goods and personal services. The personal service element is an important aspect of consumer provision in these centres. Sizes of centre range from 3000 to 10 000 m² GLA with typical centres around 5000 m². Total site area varies from 1 to 4 ha. Although some car parking space is provided, the number of spaces varies from 20, or even less, to several hundred in the larger centres. In suburban America the *key tenant* is a single supermarket in the smaller centres, but in larger centres a supermarket, hardware store and drugstore may be present. The key tenants rarely account for less than 30 per cent of GLA and this may rise to around 50 per cent when several of these key tenants or *anchors* have been built into the design. The assumed catchment population is 2500 to 40 000 people within a six-minute drive and it is generally assumed that consumers visit their nearest centre. Convenience is the merchandising concept of the neighbourhood centre. Designs vary considerably from simple shop strips to that of a fully enclosed air-conditioned building. Development is usually carried out by a small local or regionally-based developer often using relatively local funding agencies. There is great variety in the form and development of neighbourhood centres in the USA but the local nature of their catchment population is a critical feature in their definition because on this depends their convenience function and so their tenant mix and in turn the product mix and policies of the tenants. Tables 2.1, 2.2 and 2.3 summarize the key features of neighbourhood centres in America and allow comparison with community and regional centres.

The term neighbourhood centre is widely used outside the USA and although neighbourhood centres in Europe differ in detail from the American model, the basic concepts and functions are similar. The local retail function is often reinforced by the planned presence nearby, and occasionally within the centre, of local-level public service facilities such as a primary school, library and local offices of government agencies. Residential accommodation may be provided within the overall centre structure with flats built over lock-up shops. In Britain, a public house is frequently included in the centre whilst in Asian cities space for non-store retailers is often an integral part of centre design. In most New Town developments, whether in Sweden, Israel or Australia, there is a centre type which corresponds to the neighbourhood centre although it is not always called such. Centres of this type, function and size in Canberra, for

Table 2.1 Characteristics of traditional free-standing general purpose shopping centre types

MAJOR TENANT	CENTRE TYPE		
	Neighbourhood	Community	Regional
	Supermarket	Variety, discount, junior department store	Full line department store of at least 10 000 m²
Typical GLA (m²)	5000	15 000	40 000
Usual range of GLA (m²)	3000–10 000	10 000–30 000	30 000 upwards
Usual minimum site area (ha)	1	4	6
Catchment population	2500–40 000	40 000–150 000	over 150 000
Median parking ratio*	6.1	6.6	6.1
Median land cost $/m² GLA (1974)	39.8	59·7	27·5

* Parking space/100 m² GLA
Source: based on Urban Land Institute (1981, 1978, 1975)

Table 2.2 Tenant mix of traditional free-standing general purpose shopping centre types

TENANT TYPE	PERCENTAGE OF GLA			PERCENTAGE OF SALES		
	Neighbourhood	Community	Regional	Neighbourhood	Community	Regional
Retail						
Food	26.5	15.7	5.5	43.8	33.2	7.9
General merchandise	16.3	35.8	53.4	8.9	30.1	48.5
Clothing and shoes	5.5	7.8	16.9	4.2	7.6	20.4
Dry goods	3.8	3.0	1.4	1.6	2.0	1.5
Furniture	4.8	3.7	1.4	1.7	3.6	1.7
Other retail	16.9	14.5	10.1	13.4	15.5	13.3
Total retail	73.8	80.5	88.7	73.6	92.0	93.3
Services						
Food service	5.1	3.7	2.9	3.2	3.8	3.6
Personal	5.6	3.6	1.2	2.5	1.8	1.1
Financial	3.0	2.5	1.6	0	0	0
Office	4.7	2.2	0.4	0	0	1.1
Total service	18.4	12.0	6.1	5.7	6.6	5.8
Other tenants	4.7	4.3	3.0	20.7	2.4	2.0
Vacant	3.1	3.3	2.2	0	0	0

Source: Urban Land Institute (1975)

Table 2.3 Change in tenant mix by organization type in traditional free-standing general purpose shopping centre types, 1972–81

TENANT TYPE	CENTRE TYPE					
	Neighbourhood		Community		Regional	
	1972	1981	1972	1981	1972	1981
A. % tenants						
National chain	20		27		37	
Independent	58		48		35	
Local chain	22		25		28	
B. % GLA						
National chain	44	46	54	62	63	72
Independent	31	31	19	17	14	10
Local chain	25	23	27	21	23	19
C. % Sales						
National chain	55	58	57	67	62	67
Independent	20	17	15	13	11	11
Local chain	25	25	28	21	27	22
D. % Rent income						
National chain	50	37	48	52	72	59
Independent	27	38	25	24	11	18
Local chain	23	25	27	24	17	23

Source: Urban Land Institute (1972, 1981)

example, are termed *intermediate* or *group* centres but they fit well the usual definition of neighbourhood centres (Although in Canberra the term 'neighbourhood centre' has been used, misleadingly, for the very small centre type located within a small residential area.) Figure 2.1 shows the provision of shopping centres within Canberra and the location of intermediate centres serving several residential neighbourhoods. Typical is the Jamieson centre in Braddon with 5168 m² GLA divided into 24 units. Two stores, a supermarket and a general merchandise store both belonging to chain-store groups, account for 55 per cent of the floorspace and almost all the smaller units are occupied by local retailers either totally independent or operating a franchise, or service outlets.

The neighbourhood centre is a widespread shopping centre type but there is considerable variety in the detail of its form and development. Surprisingly, neighbourhood centres have received scant attention in studies of shopping centres (American Society of Planning Officials, 1955; Potter and Dowling, 1943; Villaneuva, 1945; Warren, 1973; Housing, 1980) compared with that paid to the larger centre types. Neighbourhood centres provide opportunities for small-scale entrepreneurs not only in centre development but also in retail operation and so may well be 'seedbeds' for future large commercial companies. The success or failure of individual neighbourhood centres rests largely on the commercial ability of the tenants and on the precise location of the centre. Locations embedded in residential areas tend to be favoured by land use planners but commercial developers prefer sites at intersections on major roads which are on the edge of residential blocks. These contrasts in locations are well seen between British and North American cities. Of the eleven neighbourhood centres

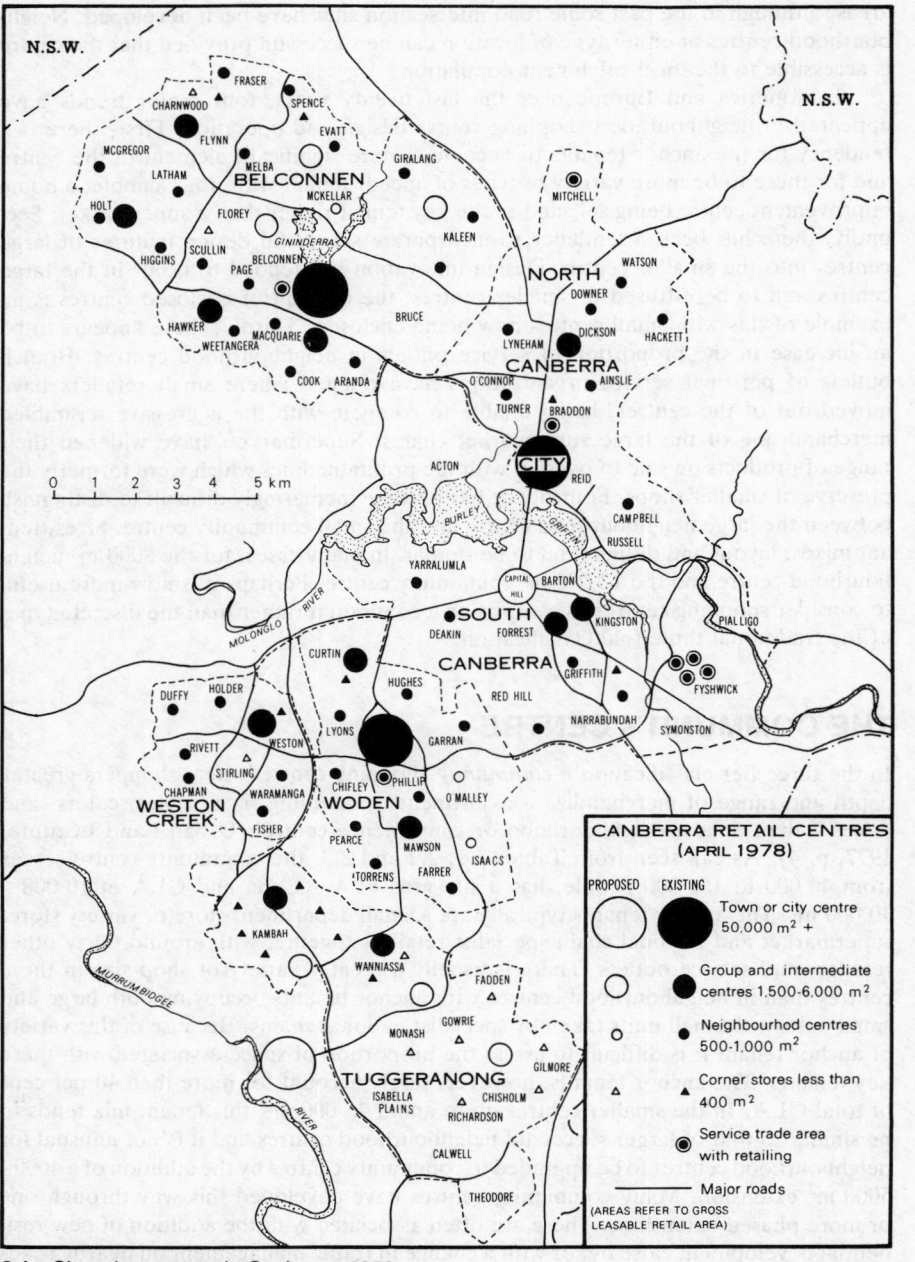

2.1 Shopping centres in Canberra, 1978.

for which construction began between June 1979 and June 1980 in Houston, Texas, for example, only one was within a residential area – the remainder were all at intersection sites on major residential distributor roads. Modern British neighbourhood centres would almost certainly not now be at such sites but would be within residential areas, although in the past some road intersection sites have been developed. Neighbourhood centres at either type of location can be successful provided that the centre is accessible to the local catchment population.

In America and Europe over the last twenty years, four major trends have appeared in neighbourhood shopping centre design and operation. First, there is a tendency for the anchor tenants to become a more significant element in the centre and for there to be more variety of types of anchor tenant with, for example, a home improvement centre being selected as the key tenant rather than a supermarket. Secondly, there has been a tendency to incorporate successful design features of large centres into the smaller centre. Design innovation has tended to occur in the large centres and to be diffused to smaller centres; the concept of enclosed centres is an example of this with small centres now being enclosed. Thirdly, there appears to be an increase in the proportion of service outlets in neighbourhood centres. Branch outlets of personal service organizations have opened where small retailers have moved out of the centres, being unable to compete with the aggressive scrambled merchandising of the large supermarket chains. Supermarkets have widened their range of products on sale to overlap with the profitable lines which were formerly the preserve of smaller shops. Fourthly, it has become increasingly difficult to distinguish between the large neighbourhood centre and the small community centre. Sizes, tenant mixes, layout and design tend to be similar, in many cases, for the 8000 m² neighbourhood centre and the 12 000 m² community centre. Perhaps it is now more useful to consider shopping centres as comprising a continuum rather than the discrete types of the traditional three-fold classification.

THE COMMUNITY CENTRE

In the three-tier classification a *community* shopping centre 'offers shoppers greater depth and range of merchandize – assortments in clothing sizes, styles, colors, and prices – than does a neighbourhood or convenience centre' (Urban Land Institute, 1977, p. 4). As can be seen from Tables 2.1, 2.2 and 2.3, the community centre serves from 40 000 to 150 000 people, has a site area of 4 – 12 ha and GLA of 10 000 – 30 000 m². The anchor tenants typically are a small department store or variety store, supermarket and national chain specialist retailers together with around thirty other retailers and service outlets. There is usually a greater variety of shop size in these centres than in neighbourhood centres with anchor tenants occupying both large and small units with small units taken by specialist national chains. Because of this variety of anchor tenant it is difficult to assess the proportion of space associated with these key tenants. The anchor tenants, however, rarely account for more than 40 per cent of total GLA. In the smaller centres up to about 15 000 m², this tenant mix tends to be similar to that of larger successful neighbourhood centres and it is not unusual for neighbourhood centres to be upgraded to community centres by the addition of a 4000 – 5000 m² extension. Many community centres have developed this way through one or more phased extensions. These are often associated with the addition of new residential development close by, or with a change in traffic management on nearby roads particularly where a freeway extension provides a potential enlargement of the neighbourhood centre catchment. Under such conditions of urban growth the community centre can be very successful but it is susceptible to strong competition from neighbourhood centres merchandising their convenience and larger, regional, centres focusing on specialized goods and services. The range of competitive pressures on the community shopping centre as a centre type is one reason for the appearance of other types of centre within this general size range (see below for discussion of speciality centres, hypermarket centres, central area extension centres, and so on).

The renewal and redevelopment of centres is a growing trend apparent in North America (see Ch. 5); the older community shopping centres are those where, in many cities, redesign is underway. The community centre was a strong feature of American suburban shopping centre development in the north-eastern cities in the 1950s and 1960s, often providing the opportunity for development companies to become established before embarking on larger major centre development in the last ten years. New development of community centres is still taking place, however, in the sunbelt cities and again is providing an opportunity for regional developers to prove themselves before moving to larger and often out-of-state projects. The community centre is an essentially American centre which is not well represented in other countries, except Australia, Canada, to a lesser extent New Zealand, and recently Japan. To function successfully the community centre requires large suburban districts. In much of Europe, metropolitan suburban expansion has tended to engulf villages and small towns which have formed the shopping districts at a community level in the intra-urban retail hierarchy. The scope for community level shopping centres of the American style has therefore been limited and this is a further reason for the emergence of other types of centre of this general size. The extensive suburban growth in Australian cities produces conditions similar to those in the American city and community shopping centres have become established in all the Australian state capitals (*Architecture in Australia*, 1969). In Perth, for example, fifteen such centres have been built as the city has grown to over 800 000 from 400 000 in the mid-1950s. The centres are associated with major junctions on the metropolitan road network or in a few cases are additions to small neighbourhood shopping districts which have quickly changed their function to meet the demands of the rapid population growth in the surrounding residential tracts (Johnston, 1973). The Japanese centres were developed mainly in the 1970s and are often related to the suburban rail network rather than the congested road system. Centre development has been mainly by the large commercial companies which have strong associations with the department store and supermarket groups who have then become the key tenants to several centres of 20 000 – 25 000 m² both in suburban Tokyo and Osaka as well as in the satellite cities in these metropolitan regions (*Japan Architect*, 1971a, 1970a; Yoshino, 1971).

In Europe a few community centres have been built usually in association with the planned decentralization of metropolitan regions. Around Copenhagen and Stockholm (*Deutsche Bauzeitung*, 1970; *Arkitektur*, 1967), for example, such centres operate successfully, whilst in Eastern European cities such as Budapest, community centres are being built at major interchange points on the main transit system. These locations tend to be in the middle suburbs and are also associated with large residential block development. Closer to the smaller end of this type, the Sugar centre in Budapest is associated with a major suburban train—city train—bus interchange and is anchored by a store of the largest retail trading enterprise in Hungary. There are plans for a further four or five such centres in the city but, compared with American ones, East and West European cities have relatively few community shopping centres.

THE REGIONAL CENTRE

The successful developers of community centres in the 1950s in America became, in many cases, the developers of *regional centres* in the 1960s and 1970s. The regional centre has a typical GLA of around 40 000 m² within a range from 3 000 m² to well over 100 000 m^2 with a few North American centres having over 200 000 m^2 of GLA – for comparison this is approximately the combined floorspace of all the shops in the Lancashire town of Blackpool. A considerable literature exists on the form, function and location of regional centres as shown in the major bibliographies on shopping centres. The Urban Land Institute (1977) *Handbook* is still the most comprehensive single source, texts by Hornbeck (1962), Redstone (1973) and Gosling and Maitland (1976) provide further examples, and useful statements on specific aspects of regional centres are provided by Schmertz (1974), the International Council of Shopping Centers (1965), Gruen (1962), Sales Management (1970), Kober (1977) and the J. Walter Thompson Company (1954). Within such a size range inevitably there is considerable variation in the form of centre and it has been suggested that the largest centres – over about 75 000 m^2 and with three or more department stores – constitute a distinct type, the *super-regional* centre (Harrison, 1968). The traditional type of regional centre 'provides shopping goods, general merchandise, apparel, furniture and home furnishings in full depth and variety. It is built around a full-line department store, with a minimum GLA of 100 000 square feet [*c.* 10 000 m^2] as the major drawing power.' Larger centres have several department stores, thus increasing the assumed consumer attraction of the overall centre. 'The normal design uses the pedestrian mall, either open or enclosed, as a connection between the major anchor stores. The mall also establishes a basic pattern for directing customer flow past supplementary tenant stores which are placed between the purposely separated majors' (Urban Land Institute, 1977, p. 7). Locations for such centres, which need catchment populations over 150 000, are at freeway and motorway intersections, particularly where arterial freeways intersect ring freeways. As new ring freeways are planned around American cities so new potential sites for regional centres are available and developers take options on such sites well in advance of either the road construction or the residential development. In San Antonio, for example, major regional centres exist at key intersections on loop 410 and close to loop 13, and there are plans for new openings in 1983 and 1984 at sites on the northern section of loop 1604. These are shown on Figure 2.2, which also shows the concentration of regional centres in the middle- and upper-income areas in the north and north-west parts of the city. This pattern is typical of many North American cities where regional shopping centres now form major suburban activity nodes with their own set of land use linkages and acting as stimulants for the general processes of commercial growth. Recent development activity has concentrated on the creation of very large centres, and also the building of small regional centres in what are termed *middle markets* or medium-sized cities where the centre will be the only regional centre in the city (Thorsen, 1974; *Shopping Center World*, 1980c; Dunham, 1981) (see Ch. 4).

Again, the expanding suburbia of Japan, Canada, Australia and South American cities (*Shopping Center World*, 1980b; Campbell, 1974) show similar development patterns although modified by local conditions. In Japan multi-level centres with relatively-low parking ratios have been built (*Japan Architect*, 1970b), whilst in Australia, particularly in the middle suburbs, land use planners have encouraged integration of regional centres into small established shopping districts. Such centres effectively become extension centres rather than true regional centres. The generally stronger land use planning legislation in Europe is one of several factors which have inhibited widespread development of regional centres; by 1981, approximately 75 regional shopping centres were operational in suburban Europe compared with the 1350 in the USA. The presence in Britain of only one such centre, Brent Cross in north London, is in large measure due to the control exerted by land use planners

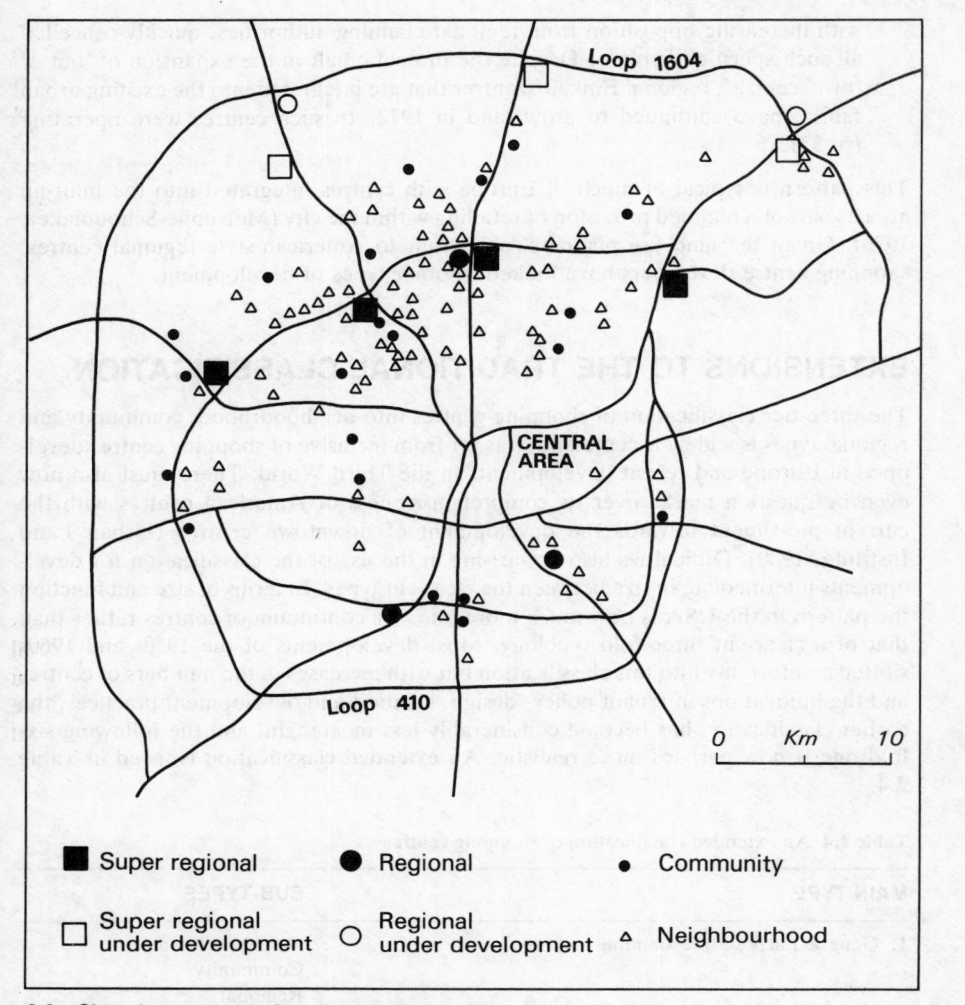

2.2 Shopping centres in San Antonio, Texas, 1981.

and their negative attitude to large-scale suburban retail development. In Germany in the mid-1960s, the scene seemed set for the rapid growth of regional shopping centres (*Business Week*, 1964; *The Economist*, 1966; Day, 1964) but regional planning authorities opposed it and the initial impetus was lost. Shaw (1978) points to the early growth in the mid-1960s and to the subsequent lack of positive activity.

The two earliest developments, of the Main-Tanus-Zentrum opened in 1964 and the Ruhrpark Zentrum in 1965, were both 'out of town' centres at some distances from the city centres. Significantly, both made use of locations close to important autobahn links which serves to increase their potential trade area. Thus, the largest of the two, the Main-Tanus-Zentrum with a total area of 70 000 m², is located some 11 km west of Frankfurt at the intersection of a number of autobahn. These two developments led to proposals for a further 81 such free-standing shopping centres to be built over a ten year period. However, in 1966 the developers, faced with increasing opposition from regional planning authorities, quickly cancelled all such speculative plans. Despite the dramatic halt in the expansion of 'out of town' centres, regional Einkaufszentrer that are integrated into the existing urban fabric, have continued to grow, and in 1972, 16 such centres were operating (p. 37).

This pattern is typical of much of Europe with centres integrated into the built-up area as part of a planned provision of retailing within the city (Merrenne-Schoumaker, 1976). Given the land use planners' objections to American-style regional centres, shopping centre developers have looked to other types of development.

EXTENSIONS TO THE TRADITIONAL CLASSIFICATION

The three-tier classification of shopping centres into neighbourhood, community and regional types is widely accepted but it is far from inclusive of shopping centres developed in Europe and recent developments in the Third World. There must also now even be question marks over its comprehensiveness of American centres with the current movement towards the development of downtown centres (Urban Land Institute, 1980). Difficulties also are arising in the use of the classification for developments intermediate in size between the clear-cut types. In terms of size and function the pattern in the USA is now much more one of a continuum of centres rather than that of a clear-cut three-fold typology. Most developments of the 1950s and 1960s slotted comfortably into this classification but with increases in the numbers of centres and the innovations in tenant policy, design, location and development practices, the earlier classification has become considerably less meaningful and the following six-fold one is now perhaps more realistic. An extended classification is listed in Table 2.4.

Table 2.4 An extended classification of shopping centres

MAIN TYPE	SUB-TYPES
1. General purpose free-standing centres	Neighbourhood Community Regional Strip Super-regional
2. General-purpose centres in shopping districts (Renewal centres)	Infill Extension Core replacement
3. Multi-use centres	New Town centres Downtown megastructures
4. Ancillary centres	Hotel-associated Office-associated Transport-associated
5. Speciality centres	Purpose-built In recycled buildings
6. Focused centres	

Table 2.5 Some characteristics of the major shopping centre types

CHARACTERISTIC	CATEGORY											
	Strip	Neighbourhood	Community	Regional	Super-regional	Infill	Extension	Core replacement	Multi-use	Ancillary	Specialist	Focused
Design												
Typical size (m²)	1500	5000	20 000	50 000	100 000	2500	15 000	40 000	40 000 (retail)	3000	6000	10 000
No. of levels	Single	Usually single	Usually single	Single or multi	Usually multi	Usually single	Usually multi	Multi	Multi	Usually single	Single or multi	Usually single
Open/enclosed	Open	Usually open	Both	Usually enclosed	Enclosed	Usually open	Usually enclosed	Enclosed	Usually enclosed	Both	Usually enclosed	Both
Management												
On-site manager	No	No	Sometimes	Usually	Yes	No	Sometimes	Yes	Yes	Sometimes	Sometimes	Sometimes
Tenant association	No	Usually	Usually	Yes	Yes	No	Usually	Yes	Usually	No	Usually	Unusually
Opportunity for small retailers	Yes	Some	Few	None	None	Yes	Some	Few	Few	Yes	Some	Few
Anchor tenant	None	Supermarket store	Variety store	Dept. store	Dept. store	None	Varied store	Dept. store	Dept. store	None none	Often none	Mass merchandiser
Control of tenant mix	Slight	Slight	Some	Considerable	Considerable	Slight	Some	Considerable	Considerable	None	Considerable	Considerable
Location												
Optimal	Close to regional regional centre	Intersection in local road network	Intersection in Intra-urban road system	Inter-urban Intra-urban freeway intersection	Inter-urban within conurbation	Close to peak land value of retail district	Close to core replacement downtown	Traditional centre of downtown	New community	Large office/hotel	High-income district	Jct. in intra-urban road network
value as growth pole	None	None	Limited	Some	Some	None	None	Considerable	Considerable	None	Limited	Limited

The traditional American suburban centre may be considered as category 1.

1. *General Purpose Free-Standing Shopping Centre* with sub-types of:
   (i) *neighbourhood*
   (ii) *community*
   (iii) *regional*

   As such it forms the basis for a broader typology to include more recent trends in centre development. The neighbourhood centre is usually considered the smallest centre type despite Hoyt's (1958) suggestion of a small neighbourhood type. There are, as Hoyt appreciated, a large number of small strip or parade developments which form a fourth sub-group of
   (iv) *strip centres*
   whilst the
   (v) *super-regional*
   may be added to the top end of the sub-types.

   There is a second major group of centres:
2. *General Purpose Shopping Centre within a Shopping District* (alternatively termed *renewal* centres) with three sub-types:
   (i) *infill centre*
   (ii) *extension centre*
   (iii) *core replacement centre*

   Alongside the general purpose shopping centres are the further categories 3–6:
3. *Multi-use Shopping Centres* in which social facilities are integrated with commercial provision as is the case in many New Town shopping centres and in some major CBD redevelopment schemes.
4. *Ancillary Shopping Centres* which provide retail floorspace within structures developed primarily for another function such as hotel, office or transport complexes.
5. *Speciality Shopping Centres* with sub-types of:
   (i) *purpose-built* speciality centres, such as fashion centres
   (ii) *recycled* speciality centres such as centres in former market halls.
6. *Focused Shopping Centres* in which a single large tenant dominates retail provision such as occurs in hypermarket-based centres.

Within any one of these centre types there is great variety of centre design with single and multi-level designs, open and enclosed centres and a range of parking ratios. Table 2.5 provides a general comparison of the different types but inevitably there is variety within each type as centres are designed by different people and are developed for different locations.

THE STRIP CENTRE AND SUPER-REGIONAL CENTRE

The *neighbourhood, community* and *regional centres*, three sub-types of category 1, have already been discussed. The *strip centre* is the most numerous centre type and is also the most international. It is small and relatively easily developed, providing commercial and investment opportunities for small businesses both in development and in retailing. Such centres may also be developed and quickly built by government agencies in response to specific locational needs. Tenants adapt their trading methods to the locality they serve which may only be within a radius of a few hundred metres of the development. Centres may be free-standing or, as is popular in the USA, on sites adjacent to large community or regional shopping centres, attempting to com-

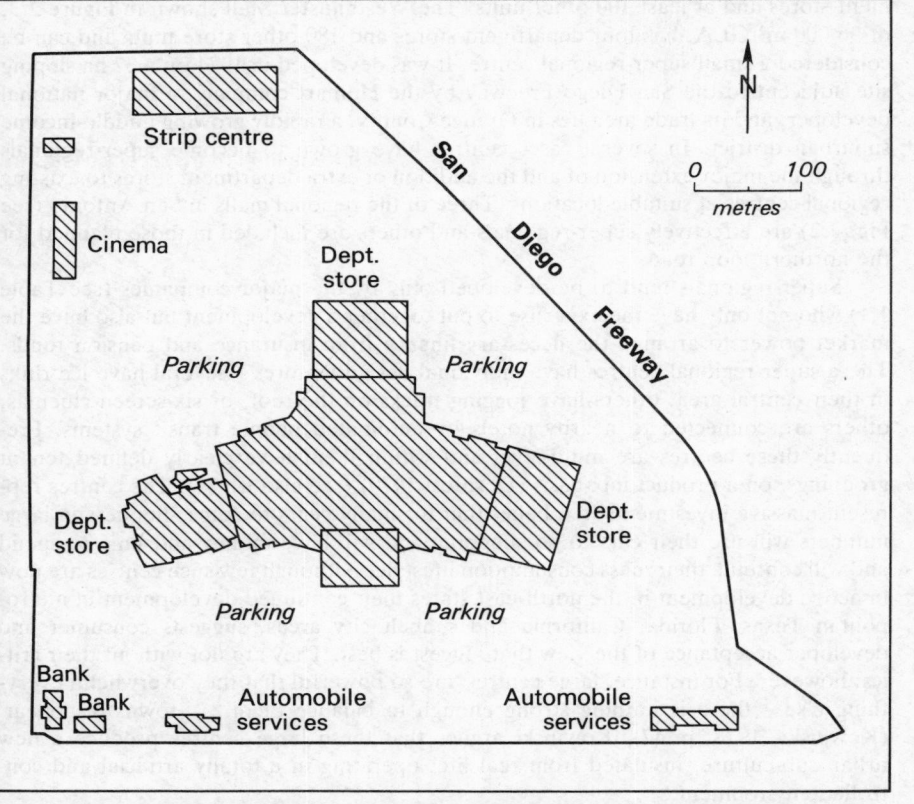

2.3 A super-regional centre in Westminster, California with a strip centre located on peripheral land.

plement the essentially *comparison goods* product mix of the large centre (Schwartz-
Barker, 1979; Opsata, 1979); Figure 2.3 shows this locational association of a strip
centre within the plot developed as a super-regional centre in suburban southern California. Tenant replacement is relatively high in strip centres and as increased competitive pressures affect small retail and service businesses in capitalist economies so
vacancies increase, but there is generally a steady supply of entrepreneurs ready to
risk investment in the development and the occupancy of these centres. In socialist
economies the mix of retail types is more tightly controlled but this type of centre is
becoming commonplace as the lowest tier in planned urban retail provision through
the world. It is also one of the few types of centre operating in rural settlements, at
least within economically developed countries. Most of the readers of this book frequently will visit such centres and the centres have become an accepted part of
society's organization of retail provision yet relatively little research has been carried
out into them.

In contrast, the *super-regional centre* is a fairly rare breed, effectively accessible
only to middle- and higher-income suburban North American consumers. By 1981
there were approximately 250 such centres over 100 000 m² in the USA and these
were all in major metropolitan regions. Such centres usually have three to six depart-

ment stores and at least 100 other units. The Westminster Mall shown in Figure 2.3, of 96 000 m² GLA, has four department stores and 180 other store units and can be considered a small super-regional centre. It was developed in 1974 on a 37 ha sloping site adjacent to the San Diego Freeway by the Homart company, a major national developer, and its trade area lies in Orange County, a rapidly growing middle-income suburban district. In several cases centres have grown to become super-regionals through the major extension of and the addition of extra department stores to existing regional centres at suitable locations. Three of the regional malls in San Antonio (see Fig. 2.2) are effectively super-regionals and others are included in those planned for the northern loop road.

Super-regionals tend to be developed only by the major companies (see Table 1.1) who not only have the expertise to put together a development but also have the market power to arrange the necessary finance from insurance and pension funds. These super-regional centres have individual design features – several have ice rinks in their central area, others have jogging tracks on the roof, or six-screen cinemas, others are connected to nearby hotels by automated people transit systems. Frequently these centres are multi-level and within them have clearly defined tenant groupings, on a product mix basis (Despres, 1970) (see also Ch. 5). The centres represent massive investments in a belief that for many years to come shoppers in large numbers will use their cars to go shopping and will have money and time to spend and will continue their mass consumption lifestyle. Although few such centres are now in active development in the north-east states their continued development in metropolitan Texas, Florida, California and sunbelt city areas, suggests consumer and developer acceptance of the view that biggest is best. They are not without their critics, however. For instance, large centres 'are so powerful that they overwhelm everything else – there is nothing strong enough to balance them . . . towns disappear' (Kowinski, 1978, p. 47). Kowinski argues that these large centres produce a new urban sub-culture, insulated from real life, operating in a totally artificial and controlled environment.

CENTRES WITHIN SHOPPING DISTRICTS

Category 1, general purpose suburban shopping centres, range from 200 m² strips to 200 000 m² super-regionals. The size range for the category 2 shopping centres within shopping districts also is large but few centres have matched the Eaton Centre in Toronto and broken the 100 000 m² barrier, largely because of the greater problems of land acquisition in city centres compared with the suburbs. Depending on the function and location of the centre it is possible to distinguish three sub-types of general purpose shopping centres within shopping districts – infill centres, extension centres and core replacement centres.

The first type, *infill centre*, usually comprises up to about 20 units built on a redeveloped site within an established shopping district. Units are frequently between 100 m² and 150 m² and occasionally one or two slightly larger units are included to meet the demands of specific tenants. Small property development companies are often responsible for these developments and the centre is developed speculatively except for the larger units, where potential tenants will have been approached by the developer and have had an opportunity to influence the design of their unit and also possibly to negotiate preferential clauses in their lease. The remainder of the units will be let on standard leases. Typical locations for these centres are behind the frontage of a major shopping street but with access to the main shopping street. They are thus in essentially secondary locations and redevelop sites given over to storage, warehousing and retailing, where economic or physical blight is present or likely. Infill centres occur in the central areas of shopping districts of small and large towns, in CBDs and in suburban business districts. Towns with a total population as small as 5000 may prove suited to such schemes whilst in large towns several infill centres may be present in the central shopping district and even in suburban shopping districts. Infill centres, together with strip centres and to a lesser extent neighbourhood centres, provide developments where progressive independent retailers can lease, at affordable rents, lock-up shops and enlarge their business. The tenant mix is not closely controlled except in a few cases where attempts are made to provide a theme or focus for the centre, but then such centres cease to be general purpose centres and become speciality centres. This form of infill centre development is widespread in North America and Europe, generally wherever property developers are active, and such development also provides a method for enhancing retail provision in a planned but piecemeal, low cost way in socialist countries. These centres are numerous. Major cities in Britain, for example, typically have several dozen such centres developed over the last thirty-five years. One aspect of the return to downtown locations for shopping centres which is apparent in the USA is the possibility of small piecemeal developments of this type starting up (McCahill, 1976). In suburban North America it is sometimes difficult to distinguish strip and infill centres but if infill centres are defined as being limited to locations within shopping districts and ribbon developments, then a distinction can be made. Within ribbon developments small infill centres are common, filling gaps in the ribbon and redeveloping portions of it. In size, design, development process and tenant mix, the strip and infill centres may be similar but they differ in location. As with strip centres, however, relatively little research has been carried out on infill centres.

The second type, *extension centre*, occurs where existing retail floorspace in a shopping district becomes insufficient to meet the demands of a growing population and expanding retail economy. The purpose of such centres is to provide more floorspace in a planned way rather than simply to redevelop small blighted parcels of land to provide better quality retail premises. None the less extension centres frequently involve the redevelopment of low rental retail and wholesaling buildings and poor quality residential property on the edge of the established shopping and commercial district. There is a considerable range of centre sizes but many are in the 7500 m^2 range so they provide in most cases a substantial addition to the existing floorspace of the shopping district. As might be expected these centres are particularly common as extensions to the central area of suburban shopping districts in expanding suburban residential areas. This is true particularly of countries where, for various reasons, development of the larger free-standing suburban shopping centres has not been allowed. In Britain, for example, land use policy has sought to contain commercial expansion to existing retail districts and extension centres provide the method by which retail floorspace was built to meet the demands of the growing suburban population of the 1950s and 1960s (see Ch. 6). The tenant mix in extension centres reflects the general trading character of the district in which it is located, but it usually contains one or two larger units for a supermarket, freezer centre or household goods shop. The anchor tenants may well be branches of national chains of specialist retailers which only require relatively small units. Tenant selection and mix is an important factor in the success or failure of these centres. In successful cases, the centre of gravity of the whole shopping district is likely to shift closer to the extension centre thus incorporating it fully into the shopping district. Failed centres, those with the wrong tenant mix or perhaps based on over-estimates of the capacity of the shopping district to absorb extra floorspace, become blighted rapidly and subject to vandalism as they are built on the periphery of the commercial district where blight and urban decay may already be widespread. It is common for a relatively high proportion of units in extension centres to be taken by service establishments. This reflects the changing functions of commercial districts and provides an opportunity for the entry of new functions without seriously affecting the existing mix in the shopping district. Several examples of centres of this type in Britain are considered in Chapter 6, but this centre type is not limited to Britain and occurs wherever there are locational constraints on free-standing centre development in an established and growing urban area.

The third sub-type of category 2 is the *core replacement centre*. Again this type varies in size depending on the size of the town but few are less than 15 000 m² and several of the larger ones which have renewed considerable sections of major cities are over 75 000 m². The purpose of these centres is to replace structurally and func- tionally obsolete retail property in prime locations with new retail space designed for contemporary retail techniques. The centres provide a new focus for central area shopping activity and can act as a revitalization pole for the whole business district. The tenant mix is comparable to regional free-standing centres and it is not unusual for retailers displaced by the scheme to relocate in the new centre. The rebuilding of town centres in bomb-damaged European cities after the Second World War provided the opportunity to develop several centres of this type which became forerunners of many more as redevelopment fever hit European planners and developers alike. Sub- sequently cities elsewhere in the world, in Japan, Australia, South Africa, began cen- tral city redevelopment schemes and in the 1970s American developers were asserting that 'Downtown is where the shopping centre industry is going' (*Shopping Center World*, 1978b, p. 34). Large, complex, core replacement shopping centres are now an active or planned part of the central business district of the majority of large American cities (De Vito, 1980; Urban Land Institute, 1980; Mayor's Commission, 1973; Kober, 1981; Spink, 1981; Spalding 1981). They have existed in many European cities for a decade or more (Smith, 1977) but their numbers are limited by the con- siderable difficulties which arise in obtaining sites of 4 ha or more in a city centre.

The most numerous form of this type is not the massive construction of 75 000 m² but schemes of 15 000–25 000 m² in the core of a suburban shopping district of a major metropolitan area or in the central shopping district of a medium-sized town. Many such centres were built in the early 1960s and had designs open to the weather but more recent centres are partially or, as is increasingly common, fully enclosed. From 50 to 150 retail and service units may be incorporated in such centres and the three or four large units probably account for 25 per cent to 40 per cent of floorspace. Typical anchor tenants leasing large units are a supermarket or hypermarket, junior department store, variety store, or household goods store, but the high level of rep- resentation of national chain retailers with top credit ratings means that some of the smaller units are let to anchor tenants (Davies and Bennison, 1980). The 100 or so centres of this type in Britain reflect activity by development companies and also by local government authorities whose help is often required for the prerequisite land consolidation.

These three sub-types of shopping centres integrated into shopping districts are distinct in terms of purpose rather than size but almost inevitably core replacement schemes are large and infill centres small. It is not unusual for cities to have devel- opments of all three types, however, just as we might expect cities to have examples of the different sub-types of free-standing suburban centre. Piecemeal redevelopment provides infill centres, whilst a central area may have expanded its retailing by extension centres and also within the last thirty years have hosted a major core replacement scheme. All three sub-types aim at providing in their tenant mix what might be termed general purpose retail provision.

MULTI-USE CENTRES

The third major category, the *multi-use shopping centres* (sometimes called mixed use centres), in contrast are, as the name suggests, developments in which retailing is part of a broader planned land use and activity mix within a single building complex (*Shopping Center World*, 1981a; Brubaker, 1975). These centres are usually large with 20 000 m² or more of retailing space together with extensive office, hotel and residential space. Retailing has a key role in these centres and is not simply a peripheral addition as in ancillary shopping centres (see p. 34). The Urban Land Institute (1977) defines multi-use centres as 'large scale, high-density urban projects characterized by physical integration of mutually supportive land uses' (p. 265) and provides the example of the Renaissance Centre on the Detroit Waterfront where four office towers, a seventy-storey hotel and 30 000 m² of retailing are combined in a single megastructure. The importance of such centres in the general economy of American central cities is stressed in the *Downtown Development Handbook* published by the Urban Land Institute (1980). In downtown Atlanta the Peachtree Centre is typical of multiuse centres in other cities and is on the northern edge of the traditional CBD core. The project spans five blocks of the city and consists of a mix of office, hotel and trade centre uses alongside 12 700 m² of retail space. Although this retail space is less than in other centres there are plans for its extension. Also, within the scheme limited retail space is directly associated with the hotel and office buildings. Five blocks west of the Centre is Omni International, another multi-use megastructure on a 13.6 ha site above railway lines. Here 19 000 m² of retailing is provided within a development of offices, a hotel and an entertainment centre. Atlanta is not alone in having such redevelopment schemes in which high-quality comparison retailing plays a significant part, nor are such schemes limited to the USA. Many of the examples provided in Redstone (1976) are of this type and the account by de Weijer (1975) of the Karregat scheme in Eindhoven shows well the need for cooperation between private enterprise and local government if the centre is to be a success in terms of all its facilities being used.

Increasingly, general purpose shopping centres are attracting non retail uses, but the primary function of these centres remains the provision of retail space. In multiuse centres the aim is to provide a balanced distribution of space amongst several activities. It is not only in American cities anxious to revamp their worn downtown areas that multi-use development occurs. New Town development, in the British New Towns, in Canberra, suburban Stockholm, Israel and even the USA, usually involves the creation of multi-use centres. The New Town shopping centre schemes in Britain, for example, have major anchor tenants of department stores, chain variety stores, hypermarkets and 100 or so other units alongside offices, recreational facilities and, frequently, residential provision all within the one centre. In Milton Keynes this is a single megastructure, but more usually it is in several linked structures. To develop centres of the size and complexity usually associated with multi-use centres it is necessary to have a quite different development process and to involve to a greater extent central government agencies. Such is the case in New Town development, in the massive CBD redevelopment schemes underway in the USA and in the few prestige centres in Third World cities (Green, 1978).

ANCILLARY CENTRES

In general purpose shopping centres, retailing is the dominant use, in multi-use developments it is of a roughly equal status as other uses and in *ancillary shopping centres*, the fourth major category, it is a minor feature in a structure designed primarily for another purpose. The tenant mix is chosen to complement the use in the rest of the building. The three most common locations for these centres are as follows:

(a) on the ground floor or basement of large office buildings with a tenant mix aimed at servicing office workers – sandwich bars, ladies' clothes shops, tobacconists, newsagent/bookshop, etc. Centres in the basements of adjoining buildings may be linked by pedestrian passages, themselves lined with stores. In Houston, Dallas, Minneapolis, Atlanta and several other large American cities an underground pedestrian network has been built linking office, hotel and public buildings in the CBD, and the basements of many of these buildings are ancillary shopping centres.

(b) associated with a hotel/tourist complex with a tenant mix aimed at both shops and services to serve the convenience needs of hotel residents (toiletries, hairdresser,

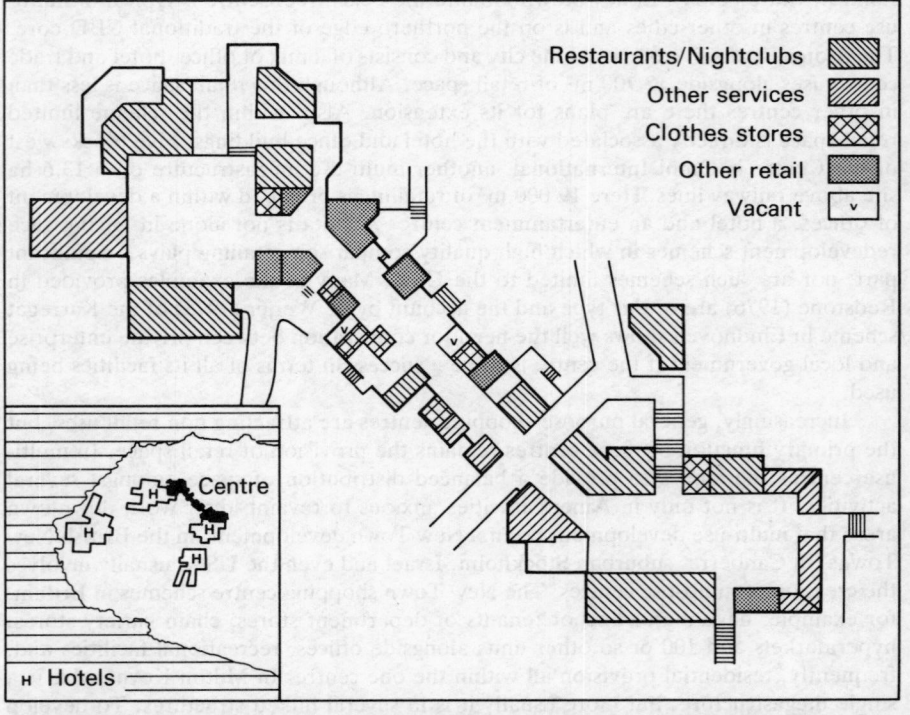

2.4   An ancillary shopping centre associated with a holiday hotel development in Dubrovnik, Yugoslavia.

quality and high fashion clothes, jewellery, cameras, etc.) and possibly to sell ethnic or cultural arts and crafts. In resort complexes which include self-catering accommodation, supermarkets, food shops and restaurants may also be included in such centres (see Fig. 2.4).

(c) associated with a transport complex, particularly mass transit interchanges, with a tenant mix providing for convenience needs of the pedestrians who pass in high flows through the centre and also including shops to allow workers returning home to buy food and other essential items.

The amount of retail space depends, to a considerable extent, on the scale of the dominant activity; there are centres of 15 000 m^2 associated with major hotel/resort complexes on the Mediterranean but also there are centres of less than 1000 m^2 with perhaps six or eight shops and kiosks in one hotel. Unit size also varies considerably but generally it is small and opportunities exist for independent retailers. The development process of these centres is subsidiary to that of the financially dominant element of the overall project. In some cases the retail space is considered as an attractive additional element in a project which must be assessed in financial terms on its office space. Ancillary centres exist in several large American CBDs and are sometimes linked by pedestrian subways. These subway schemes are usually only open during office hours and link the retail centres in the basements of the office blocks. The ancillary shopping centre in an office block is not a new phenomenon nor is it limited to downtown USA. Several examples in London were built in the immediate post-war period and centres exist in any city where office growth has occurred in the last decade, such as Sydney, Rio de Janeiro, Singapore, Tokyo (*Japan Architect*, 1971b, 1973) and also centres are being incorporated into suburban office park developments. A similarly broad pattern exists with the ancillary centres in hotels; they are included in downtown prestige hotels and in coastal resort complexes from Yugoslavia and Hong Kong to Miami and Honolulu.

SPECIALITY CENTRES

There are two remaining categories in the typology and in both retailing is dominant, but in different ways. The *speciality centre* is a relatively recent growth phenomenon, although its origins can be traced back to the fashion arcades in European cities of the nineteenth century, and it has evolved rapidly in two directions. First, there are purpose-built theme centres in which the tenant mix is very carefully controlled and limited to a restricted range of high quality and usually high price goods. Typical are centres concentrating on fashion goods. These centres may include a small department store and gourmet food shops, but more usually the majority of tenants are limited to fashion clothes, jewellery and accessories (*National Mall Monitor*, 1981; *Progressive Grocer*, 1965; *House and Home*, 1974; Scott and Gammie, 1979). Usually located in high-income suburban areas these centres may develop a city-wide trade area. Centres may focus on other merchandise themes such as art and antiques or products from a particular country and a recent trend has been to develop centres containing shops selling goods directly from the factory (*Shopping Center World*, 1980a). There are usually restaurants, and personal and specialist services such as an art insurance broker or a freight forwarding agency may be included, as may manufacturing jewellers, in the fashion centre. Generally units are small and tenants are long-established independents or small specialist chains. The success of such centres depends on accurate assessments of consumer segmentation and also on the design of the centre. Poor design may repel potential consumers visiting an art-based speciality centre. Centre developers need to know local conditions well and major national development companies may avoid such centres as they have a relatively high failure rate.

The second sub-type of *speciality centre* is that developed in renovated and refurnished old buildings which have architectural merit. The numbers of such centres are not great but their influence on the shopping centre industry outweighs this (Hoyte, 1975; Dean, 1977). Covent Garden in London, Ghiradelli Square in San Francisco, Faneuil Hall in Boston and the Rocks Centre in Sydney, are all well known centres of this type but many smaller examples were developed in the 1970s (Whitehall, 1977; Hall, 1980; Stenning, 1980; Wacher and Flint, 1980). Generally such centres cater for specialist retailers, operating out of small units and within some broad thematic framework. Often this is a focus on hand crafted goods to meet the demands of the growing segment of environmentally aware consumers but other themes are possible and may be taken from the original use of the building, which may be a railway station, warehouse, market hall or factory. Centres are generally small with few over 5000 m² and with a small size of unit. An upper limit on centre size of 10 000 m² seems likely to be the case; at about this size shop numbers will be too great to sustain the necessary centre image. Development of these centres, often either in very high rent commercial sections of a city or in the rundown CBD fringe, usually needs governmental assistance either as an initial catalyst or as a longer-term continuous input into development and management.

FOCUSED CENTRES

The sixth and final main centre type is the *focused centre* where a single tenant operates from a large unit which totally dominates centre structure. The dominant tenant may account for as much as 90 per cent, but more usually around 70 per cent, of GLA with a half dozen or so small units constituting the remaining space. The most common dominant tenant in this centre type is the hypermarket. Early centres date from the mid-1960s but since the mid-1970s a few centres have been developed with other dominant tenant types, particularly household furniture stores, discount department stores or hardware/do-it-yourself stores. Locations for these centres may be within established shopping districts or at free-standing sites in the suburbs. Centres are seldom less than 3000 m² GLA or larger than 15 000 m². Below 3000 m² the large store is not large enough to act as a customer attraction without the support of other large stores, and above 15 000 m² the large discount or convenience store is reaching a size where diseconomies of scale are increasingly prevalent. The smaller units in these stores are leased to retail and service outlets which complement the merchandise mix in the dominant store. Financial services, a dry cleaner, fresh food stores and a tobacconist are typical tenants of the smaller units, but the exact mix depends on the dominant tenant.

The early evolution of this centre type took place in France during the 1960s as hypermarkets moved away from the idea of a single store on a site. By introducing a limited amount of complementary retailing the attraction of the hypermarket was increased and consumers used the new centre for 'one-stop' shopping. The subsequent development of the concept took place notably in France and in Britain but by the early 1980s development was widespread through Europe with about 500 such centres, and some large North American retailers were experimenting with this type of centre in the USA and Canada. It is not unusual for the dominant tenant to act as the developer of the centre so controlling the tenant mix and using the large companies' high credit rating to raise development funds. These centres, and their recent rapid growth, are considered in more detail in Chapter 6.

The six-fold classification of centres with their sub-types presented in this chapter seeks to provide a more comprehensive typology than that given by the division into neighbourhood, community and regional centres. The new typology, summarized in Table 2.5, is still not totally comprehensive but it can be used as a framework for the analysis of the vast majority of centres in the world. In most classification exercises in urban geography, types merge with each other as change in social and economic structure occurs. This is certainly the case with shopping centres where it is possible for a particular centre to change its character through redesign and an evolving tenant mix. Within each centre type there inevitably exists variation. Centres are scattered about a norm and each centre responds through management decisions to the conditions of its location.

In many cities examples of all six types have been developed. Figure 2.2 shows the range of general purpose free-standing centres in San Antonio, Texas, a city of about one million population, but it excludes the many small strip centres. Within the downtown area plans are advanced for a major core-renewal project with an anticipated opening in 1984. This involves finance from central government acting as the catalyst for national developer involvement (see Ch. 3). Within the downtown area there are two renovated specialist centres focusing on craft products and owing much to local government stimulus. Some of the new community shopping centre development is moving towards the focused centre concept with a single dominant large discount superstore and a handful of small tenants. This wide range of centre types is now typical of large North American and Australian cities. In Europe the free-standing general purpose centres are less common but there still exists a considerable range of centres.

The main concern of the description of centre types in this chapter has been the form, function and related tenant mix of the centres. Development processes also differ amongst centre types and the next chapter considers in more detail these processes and the decision making which occurs to bring centres into existence.

CHAPTER 3
THE SHOPPING CENTRE DEVELOPMENT PROCESS

The creation of shopping centres is a complex and time-consuming operation. Rarely does it take less than two years of intensive negotiation and construction to develop even a small centre and in some cases the development process may take twenty years or more. The Brent Cross centre in North London took from the late 1950s to 1976 to develop with delays which were often attributed to the much-maligned British land use planning system. The infamous Bridewater Commons Centre in New Jersey dating from 1962 has been more than twenty years in gestation and may yet be stillborn with a history of complex litigation and complicated commercial dealing. For the purpose of this chapter the development process is considered to be the activities and relationships amongst interested institutions in the period between the initial idea to create a shopping centre and the centre's opening for trading.

At the core of the development process are the executive bodies of:

(a) developer;
(b) designer/architect;
(c) environmental, usually land use, planner;
(d) property consultant.

These were summarized in Figure 1.3. Generally in the USA only the environmental planner is a government employee, but in Britain local government may be the employer of any or all the other three groups whilst in socialist economies the entire process is carried out by government departments. Clearly, then, relationships amongst these four will differ depending on whether they are individual companies operating within an individual corporate plan with corporate aims, or whether they are government departments responsible to an elected body. Although relationships amongst the four groups are different the basic function of each of the four is the same, irrespective of country and society.

DECISIONS TO INITIATE A SCHEME

Initially it is usually the developer who perceives the potential demand for a shopping centre and decides whether or not to pursue the idea. The idea may result from some perceptive thinking by the developer about future demand; it may come through an approach by a major retailer who wishes to expand into an area, or it may come from a government agency wishing to build up service provision in an area; if the developer is a government agency, the idea may simply be the execution of an established plan.

The developer has to decide on whether to proceed with the idea, by making the following judgements:

(i) by determining [that] the trade area could support a shopping centre; (ii) by determining the size and character of a shopping centre required to serve the trade area most effectively; (iii) by evaluating all available plots of ground suitable for such a development; and (iv) by selecting the land most nearly conformed to the requirements for the development of a centre of the size and character indicated by the research and that most nearly fulfilled the criteria of economic feasibility (Applebaum, 1970, pp. 168 – 9).

The steps seem reassuringly simple but considerable technical analysis is required at each step (Birnkrant, 1970).

The first step requires market surveys of the trade area and of the purchasing power within that area. Essentially inductive fact-gathering research is required to review the present position and to consider recent changes in numbers, income, mobility, buying patterns, etc. of the population and the dynamics of existing centres – number, size, location, tenant mix, prosperity, etc. Both area research, dealing with aggregate data, and consumer research, dealing with individuals, are required. The techniques of this type of research are reviewed in studies in Roca (1980). Having established the present position and recent changes, it is also necessary to calculate future patterns within the trade area. Population forecasts, income forecasts, new centre building, planned roads, etc. provide the basis for an overall forecast of the centre potential for the trade area over a three-, five- and ten-year period. The developer may at this stage drop the proposal for a centre or may move on a further step in the evaluation procedure.

The second step involves more detailed market research of a deductive kind which assesses the trade area as a potential support for different types of centre. This second stage analysis will probably rework the initial market research material and determine in more detail primary, secondary and tertiary trade area zones from which, together, 85 per cent – 90 per cent of the sales of the centre will originate. Competing centres will be assessed. The proposed centre's estimated sales potential may be calculated in this way and from this the GLA may be determined, either in a general way by the simple application of sales : floorspace ratios in existing centres, or through more sophisticated models of different potential tenant mixes and their associated sales to floorspace relationships. Figure 3.1 summarizes the activities of the first two stages.

The third step involves the search for a suitable site within the general location provided in the trade area analysis. Sites may already be owned by the developer, government agency or the retailer initiating the proposal or options to purchase may have been taken out on likely sites. Lion (1976) in his account of the centre development process in the USA suggests that little real choice may exist at this third stage given the highly competitive nature of site acquisition.

Thus many major developers, major chains, a number of real estate firms and other companies have established land banks by buying diverse parcels of land, by taking out options in strategic locations, or on a speculative basis. Some of the land may be earmarked by a chain for future development of outlets, or by a developer for a new shopping centre. It may have been acquired by a chain for defensive purposes . . . Other acquisitions of real estate are strictly speculative (p. 12).

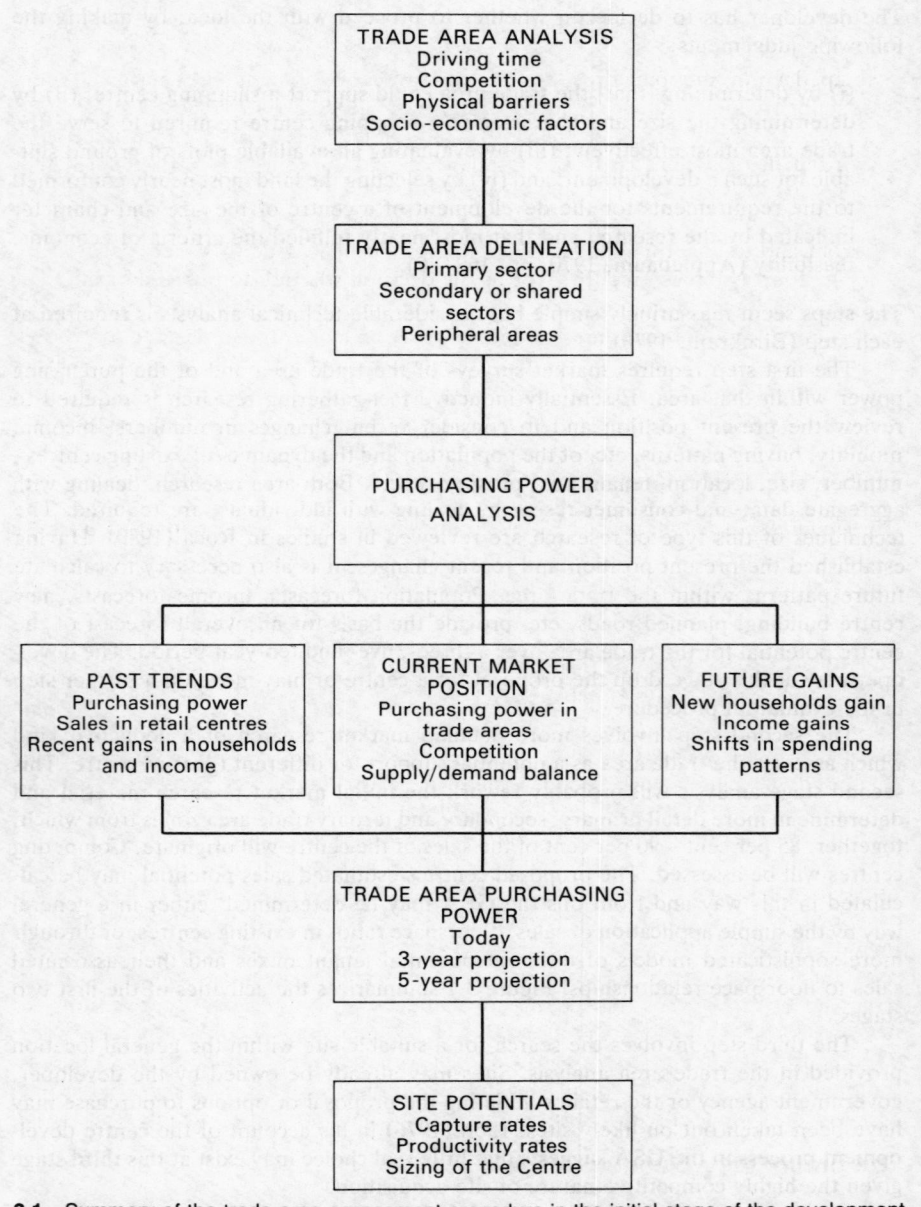

3.1 Summary of the trade area assessment procedure in the initial stage of the development process.

Although it is useful to establish the optimum site, which will be large, suitable from a construction engineering viewpoint and accessible to the defined trade area, it is not always available. Gruen and Smith (1960) considered in detail the attributes of different types of site in respect of shape, size, relationship to road network, etc. but concluded in a later study (Gruen, 1973) that 'Experience in the last twenty years has shown that many obstacles concerning difficult site problems can be overcome by planning and construction techniques' (p. 51). This is particularly true for centres developed within shopping districts where urban redevelopment takes place and there is virtually no choice of site. If alternative sites are available then cost analyses may be prepared for the more likely sites. The optimal site may be more expensive to obtain but development costs and ultimate operating profits may offset the higher initial costs (Bennett, 1971). A cost-benefit analysis is possible for alternative sites and is applicable equally to developments where the benefits come to the developer via profit and to governmental schemes where benefits accrue to society generally.

The fourth step essentially involves the decision whether to proceed or not. The prerequisites to the development – suitable location, site and entrepreneurial motivation – are all present and the final decision may be made. If it is decided to proceed then the remaining phases of the development process after the *prerequisite phase* may be termed: *planning phase*; *construction phase*; and *opening phase*.

THE PLANNING PHASE

The *planning phase* may itself be divided into three stages – an exploratory stage, a preliminary stage and a final stage. It is in the planning phase that the property consultant, environmental planner and architect take positive roles in the development process.

The exploratory planning stage

This involves initial contacts between the developer and the three professional groups which will be involved. Initial thoughts on tenant type and design will be discussed and the various planning, building and environmental permissions will be considered. A development team is effectively created who will change the original idea into a workable plan. In this exploratory stage, initial contacts will be made with finance agencies, which can be insurance companies, banks, government, likely key retailers in the scheme or any of a range of other local, national or international finance agencies. The length and complexity of discussions in this stage can range from only a few days for a small neighbourhood centre to a year or more for a major city centre core-renewal project. If the developer is not the site owner exploratory activity will take place on site acquisition. Contacts with land use planning agencies will allow, at this stage, an assessment of the likelihood of obtaining the necessary permissions for development. (See Chapters 4, 5 and 6 for a fuller discussion of the planner's role.) The result of the exploratory phase will be a *feasibility report* which defines the basic programme and pinpoints any insurmountable difficulty which will cancel the project and indicates whether it is feasible to proceed to the preliminary stage.

The preliminary planning stage

The purpose of the preliminary phase is to clarify all planning and programming factors to such a degree that a reliable economic projection can be made concerning capital cost, operating and maintenance cost and revenue. A further aim is to obtain at least approval in principle for the project from all authorities. At the end of the preliminary phase it should also be possible to enter into negotiations concerning leasing of major elements of the centre. For this purpose, it will be necessary at the end of the preliminary phase to design and publish a descriptive brochure (Gruen, 1973, p. 57).

This stage constitutes the main planning stage when the four executive participants in the development process use their own skills and draw on support teams to:

(a) prepare details of the financing of the centre;
(b) prepare a tenant mix strategy;
(c) design the centre layout including assessments of its environmental effects.

Finance

The feasibility report and market research reports for a proposed centre allow potential financiers initially to assess projects. The financing of shopping centres is extremely complex and in this aspect of the development process there is considerable difference amongst countries. Public money is frequently invested in centre development, particularly when the developer is a governmental agency. So in Britain, for example, many central area shopping centres have a financial input from the local government authority. Effectively lending money to oneself is not always considered good commercial practice and there have to be stringent legal procedures to monitor such activity. Government involvement in financing centres – particularly central area centres – is widespread and is not limited to centres where governmental agencies are developers. In the USA, six federal government financial aid schemes are available to provide some degree of financing (Leibowits, 1981). Three schemes, the Urban Renewal Program, the Community Development Block Grants and the Urban Initiation Program of the Urban Mass Transit Administration, are now relatively minor sources. In the past the Urban Renewal Program provided funds for major projects – $18 million for one development in Philadelphia. Community Development Block Grants for centres have been small and concentrated on local facilities for under this scheme centres compete for funds with local social projects. The Urban Initiation Program is a new scheme which promises to be a likely source of finance for ancillary shopping centres associated with transport facilities, but how the Program will emerge in Reaganite America remains to be seen. The three major federal aid programmes of use for centre finance are the Urban Development Action Grants from the Department of Housing and Urban Development (HUD), the grants from the Economic Development Administration (EDA) and the tax benefits associated with enhanced depreciation rates allowed on Historic Rehabilitation Projects. These are discussed in more detail than is possible here in the Urban Land Institute's *Downtown Development Handbook* (1980).

Urban Development Action Grants provide direct government money to specific projects. Both grants and loans have been supplied to central city shopping schemes, usually only on schemes where private financing has also been secured. That way, in theory at least, public money is not provided for totally non-viable projects. Grants and loans have been supplied to several cities including $2.35 million for a scheme in Cleveland and major funding for a scheme in San Antonio where HUD funding was the catalyst required for involvement by the developer, the De Bartolo Corporation. The EDA schemes provide funds for public amenities which may be integral to centre plans. In Columbus, Ohio, a public ice rink has been provided as part of a mixed use centre and many cities have had smaller projects which have enhanced the commercial viability of central city redevelopment. Thirdly, the enhanced depreciation rates on investment in some speciality shopping centres allow capital costs to be depreciated over five years for tax purposes. Again, this scheme acts as a catalyst for speciality centre development in historic buildings. Federal government finance is relatively · minor within the general financing of shopping centres in the USA, but it is a significant factor in assessing the financial feasibility of central city renewal schemes where the more traditional lenders are somewhat circumspect (*Architectural Record*, 1979).

The more traditional sources of centre finance, not only in the USA, are the insurance companies, pension funds, major banks and property investment trusts. The status of the shopping centre as a borrower has increased steadily over the last thirty years and it currently enjoys prime position in the view of many lending agencies. Cleary, a Vice-President of the Teachers' Insurance and Annuity Association, one of the top lenders to the shopping centre industry in the USA, suggested that in the 1950s 'the shopping center was not accepted as an investment vehicle by the insurance industry', but said that by the late 1970s 'the shopping center has now become the Cadillac of the lending industry. There have been fewer defaults and problems with the regional shopping center than with any other type of mortgage. And I think that this became much more noticeable during the recession of 1973 – 74' (Cleary, 1981, p. 298). Cohen's (1972) study of major mall diffusion in the USA showed the import-ance, in the initial spread of centres, of local finance and the investment returns on different property types. As shopping centre credit rating improved, so national finan-cial institutions became more involved in providing development funds and other fac-tors became important in explaining the diffusion of centres. Even with national institutional lending sources, however, there remain differences in investment yields from developments in different cities.

This lack of uniform investment returns results mainly from differentials in centre operating costs through variations in labour, energy, etc. costs and in the competitive conditions, the density of centre provision, population and income dynamics, etc. One of the reasons for the 1970s expansion of centre development in sunbelt USA was the higher investment return on centres in the south-west states compared with centres in northern cities. For example, total centre maintenance expenses per m^2 of GLA on a typical large regional centre in the south-west are half those for a northern centre and a third of those for a typical centre in a city in the mid-west. Such differences ultimately are reflected in the investment return expected from development finance. Table 3.1 shows the investment yields in major Australian cities in 1978. The higher yield in major centres in Brisbane reflects the comparative lack of such centres at the time. The higher yields for neighbourhood centres are due to their lower status as investments and the higher interest rates on development finance. These higher rates, coupled with considerable growth in neighbourhood centre development to provide for expanding suburbs, result in comparatively high yields. The Table also shows yields for other investments than shopping centres. Averaged over the cities, net

Table 3.1 Investment yield percentages from property development in Australian cities in 1978

INVESTMENT TYPE	CITY				
	Sydney	Melbourne	Adelaide	Brisbane	Perth
Neighbourhood centres	8½–10½	9–10	10–11	10	10–10½
Major centres	7½– 8½	9–10½	8	9–10	8¼
Prime city offices	6½– 7½	7½– 8½	8– 8½	7½– 8½	8
Suburban offices	9–10½	10–11	10–11	9½–10½	10
Single tenant warehouse/ industrial units	9–10	10–11	10–11½	10–11	10–10½

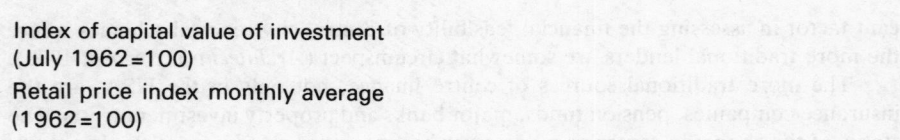

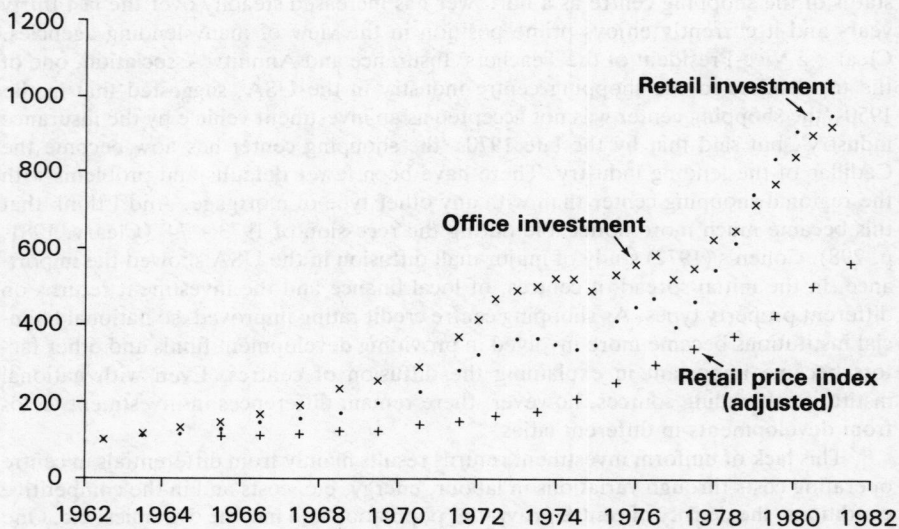

3.2 Change in the capital value of shop, office and industrial investments in Britain, 1962–82.

income growth from shopping centre investment rose from an index value of 100 in 1971 to 220 in 1976, whilst over the same period Australian consumer prices index rose similarly from 100 to 174. With such growth it is not surprising that investors did not perceive major centres, at least, as being less credit worthy than other more traditional investment types.

Investment yield is one of several aspects of interest to a potential lender. Change in capital value is another, and in this respect also shopping centres have come of age. Figure 3.2 shows the change in capital value for shop and office investments in Britain and is based on data from the Economist Intelligence Unit. Whilst this data includes all shop investment, not just that in shopping centres, it serves to illustrate the importance of retail investment to financial institutions. The retail price index is included for comparison and property investment yield can be seen to have grown considerably faster than inflation since 1962. The improvement in the credit rating of centres and the more sophisticated market analyses by investors mean that shopping centres have become very popular as investment outlets for the large financial institutions. Apart from the economic strength of centres as investments riding out a recession, there are two other related reasons for the attractiveness of centres as loan investments (Smith, 1959; Graham, 1966; Shinehouse, 1962). The first was summarized by Lisle (1981). 'It is indeed one of the attractive features to the investor that shopping is not as vulnerable to change as other sectors of investment and there is a far greater flexibility in use' (p. 45). There is always a range of tenants anxious to be represented in a successful shopping centre and the investment does not hinge therefore on the success or otherwise of a single firm. Secondly, the intensive ongoing management operation inherent in a large shopping centre operation provides a constant reassurance to the investor that fluctuations in trade in the centre can be controlled and declines reversed.

The major financial institutions may advance money for the development of the centre in several ways. The conventional mortgage is probably still the most common for small centres, with terms ranging from twenty-five to thirty-five years, but it is used increasingly less frequently with large centres requiring massive financial support. More common now are participatory mortgages where the lender supplies a partial mortgage and at the same time becomes a partner in the whole scheme. Profits from the centre operation are shared by the partners – usually the developer and lender – and mortgage payments by the developer are reduced. In such joint venture schemes the developer provides expertise and the lender provides money. Active involvement of lenders in this way can introduce a fifth institution into the executive core of the development process shown in Figure 1.3. There is considerable variety in the way joint venture schemes work, with different finance institutions assuming different levels of activity in the overall development process.

There are a number of alternatives to financing shopping centre development by using government funds or by entering into mortgage arrangements with large financial institutions. Because the major financial groups tend to be 'followers and not leaders – we don't instigate projects, we don't innovate' (Cleary, 1981, p. 297), so new types of centre tend to require other approaches to financing. Traditional finance sources are showing more interest than formerly in less conventional and párticularly in small centres (Reinsdorf, 1981; *Shopping Center World*, 1981b) but generally the large institutions and foreign investors (Opsata, 1981) prefer to invest in the types of centre which they know have produced good returns in the past. Hence the use of government funds rather than traditional private funds for city centre schemes and historic building renovation. In some focused centre development, for example, the major retailer involved acts as the developer and raises development finance via the retail company partly using operating profits and partly raising money in conventional ways (Spring, 1976). British and French hypermarket centres have been modern examples of this but the 1930s department store branch-based centres around American cities also used this method to raise development money. In a few speciality centre schemes the tenants provide development capital by purchasing a share of the centre as a way around the unwillingness of traditional finance houses to advance mortgages on relatively unconventional centre types.

Within Western capitalist society, therefore, different centre types are typically financed in different ways. Amongst the traditional free-standing centre types, private institutional finance is frequent whereas larger developments look toward national or international agencies for development money and small strip centres are more likely to depend on finance from agencies based in the local city or region. With centres within shopping districts, a similar pattern holds but government is more likely to be involved, either providing partial grants or loans, or becoming a partner in the scheme, or underwriting development costs. With mixed use developments, both large city centre schemes and smaller developments in completely new settlements, government involvement in financing development may be critical. With large and complex development schemes a complex financing operation has to be mounted. The *Downtown Development Handbook* (Urban Land Institute, 1980) explores finance problems in detail and Figure 3.3, from this source, shows a typical complex finance arrangement for a central city mixed use centre. The centre, developed by the Stouffer organization in Dayton, Ohio, incorporated a hotel within the scheme which is adjacent to a city-developed convention centre. Federal and private funds were combined

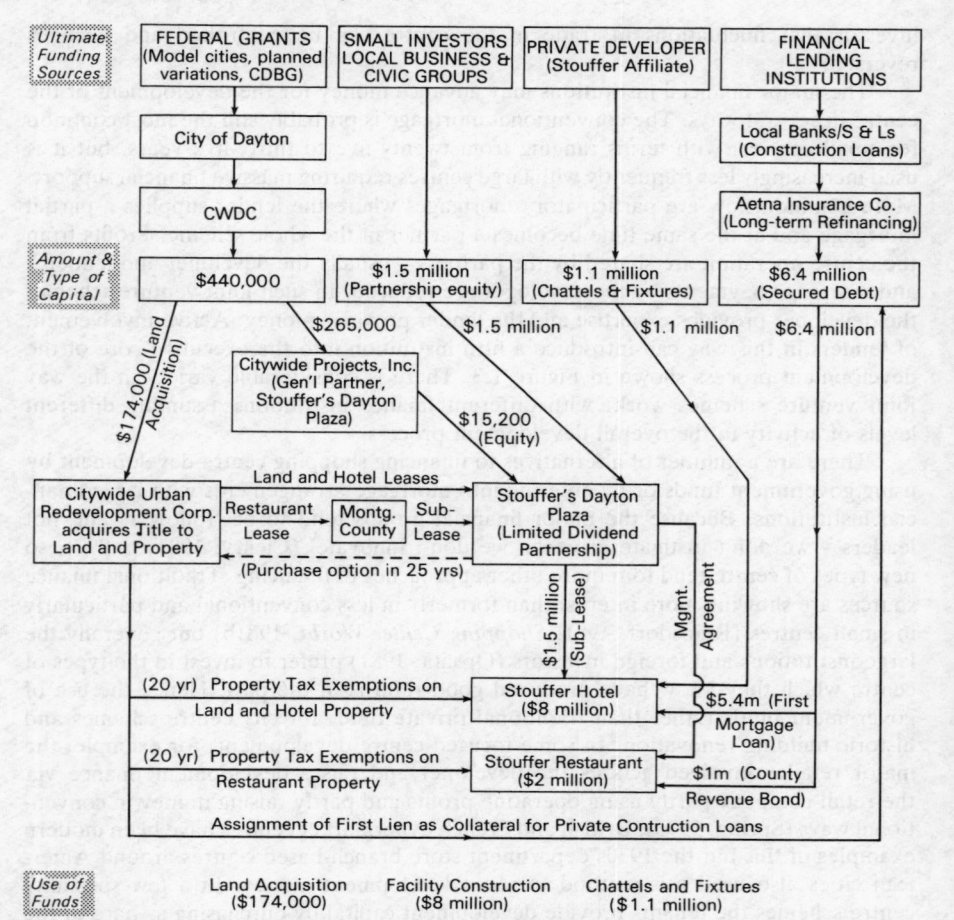

3.3 The framework of the financial plan for a mixed use centre in the CBD of Dayton, Ohio.

in a complicated financial plan to develop the centre. With other, newer centre types, then, finance schemes are less conventional and vary greatly from centre to centre. The assessment of financial sources and the arrangement of development finance is only one of the three major activities underway in the preliminary stage of centre planning.

Tenant mix

The second major activity is determining the tenant policy and tenant mix for the proposed centre. It has already been seen in the previous chapter that different centre types have quite different tenant mixes. This is no accident nor is it the result of unfettered market processes but is due to the conscious policy of the centre developer and the property consultant. The tenant mix can be defined as 'the relationship of tenants to each other in the centre as measured by:

(a) the proportion of floorspace and/or number of units of each retail and service type;

(b) the relative locations within the centre of units of different retail and service type.'

The characteristics of retail type which are relevant to decisions on tenant mix in a centre are:

- organizational form – chain, cooperative, franchise, etc.
- financial strength – credit rating, reserve backing, etc.
- sales technique – self-service, department store, catalogue show room etc.
- size of shop unit – department store of 15 000 m², kiosk 2 m², etc.
- commodity mix – food, non-food, comparison, convenience, etc.
- price: quality relationship – high price/high fashion, low price/impulse, etc.
- advertising level – special advertising needs, advertising compatability, etc.
- merchandising ability – ability to act as market leader, awareness of merchandising methods, etc.
- specific features of trading – generates litter, smells, requires special security, etc.

The tenant mix in a centre will vary with the centre characteristics of:
- centre type – strip, multi-purpose, etc.
- centre design – enclosed, multi-level, etc.
- centre location – freeway intersection, city centre, etc.
- retail environment – New Town, shopping district, major metropolitan region, etc.
- customer profile – social-economic character of trade area, ethnicity, etc.

The property consultant is required to balance these many variables and to prepare a tenant mix plan for the proposed centre. This plan is subject to an overall constraint that the tenant mix must be commercially viable and generate rent returns such that the centre development operation is ultimately profitable.

A number of general principles govern the basic tenant mix policy. First, certainly for the larger centres, 'the backbone of the entire project is its vertebrae of long term leases with strong national chain tenants which structure its financing. This basic strength, meat and potatoes, makes it possible for the developer/investor to enjoy the cake and ice cream of highly lucrative leases with smaller merchants' (Roberts, 1973, p. 624). Security and stability in the tenant mix is provided by the national chain store representation but a centre filled with such nationally known tenants is unlikely to be totally successful. The image of a centre to the customer is generated to a considerable extent by the tenant mix, and image differentiation is important in attracting customers. A centre in Bolton in the north-west of England, packed with national chains, will appear to the consumer very similar to one in Bromley to the south of London, similarly tenanted. This may not be important as the centres are not in competition, but if other centres, for example in Bury and Bexley which would be in competition with Bolton and Bromley respectively, are similarly tenanted, then the individual centre image is lost and the customer believes all centres to be the same. The inclusion of some local retailers within a centre is a common method of producing a distinct image which might allow the customer to perceive as different the otherwise similar centres in Bexley and Bromley. Certainly within the North American and Australian shopping centre industry this tenant policy is widely used, and the 'local' flavour is provided by either strong local independents, or small local chains or clearly local operators of a national franchise. Independent retailers in a large centre, however, can pose problems as business failure rates tend to be higher amongst this group.

In the larger centres developed in the 1950s and 1960s there tended to be a policy to minimize independent and local retailer involvement in centres. Competition amongst centres was not fierce and tenant selection techniques were such that national chains were solid and, as Roberts suggests, provided the 'meat and potatoes' for the developer and his family. This apparent discrimination against independent retailing was the subject of several studies and resulted in considerable controversy in several countries even to the extent of governmental intervention under various fair-trading legislation and competition acts (Cooper, 1973; Foster, 1967; Institut Français du Libre Service, 1973). Mallen and Savitt (1978) point out, however, that 'The very essence of an "organized" shopping centre is the existence of some central control over its operation, particularly control over the tenant and merchandise mix. Indeed "controlled and orderly competition" (perhaps a euphemism for restraint of trade) is given as a prime advantage of locating in a shopping centre to tenants fortunate enough to get in' (p. 27). Increased inter-centre competition, brought about by such factors as the industry's expansion, the emergence of new types of centre, governmental intervention and small retailer lobbying, has resulted in more variety in the types of retail tenants in shopping centres. Amongst the newer centre types the concentration on major national chains is not the cynosure of tenant policy, although true independents are unlikely to be able to afford or obtain access to centre units. There are many cases where independent traders open a branch in a shopping centre, are successful and open more branches, thus becoming a small chain. This improves their credit rating, extends their retail experience and consequently allows them easier entry into shopping centre tenant plans. Almost inevitably the successful independent becomes a chain store organization and so the first tenant mix policy guideline that leasing to chain stores is inevitable for a successful centre becomes self-perpetuating.

The second general policy guideline relates to the affinity, or otherwise, of store types. In shopping districts, rather than shopping centres where no formal tenant policy exists, studies (for example, Guthrie, 1980; Stambaugh, 1978) have shown that clusters of particular shop types emerge because mutual proximity increases sales, while in other shop types sales are maximized by eschewing shops of the same type. In most shopping districts also, sales are closely related to the volume of pedestrian traffic passing the shop. Shop location within centres is controlled by the tenant mix policy and lessons learnt from location in shopping districts are usually incorporated into tenant policy. The basic rule is that tenant location should be such as to maximize interaction between shop units.

In the larger centres there are four main shop types which benefit from being clustered together. First, there are men's stores – selling shoes, clothing, sports goods, etc. Secondly, grouping together shops selling women's and children's clothing, shoes and toys allows easy comparison of style, colour, price, etc. which is necessary to the pre-purchase evaluation of these types of goods. Thirdly, there are often advantages in grouping together food retailers – butcher, fishmonger, delicatessen, bakery, etc. – for consumer convenience and to increase sales volumes. Finally it is also usual to group together the personal services (dry cleaners, banks, etc.) at a location very close to the parking area or centre entrance. In some centres, a separate building within the parking area is provided for these tenants, which allows consumers quick and easy access and also, with enclosed centres, enables these tenants to operate outside normal trading times.

There are some shop types which benefit from separation within the centre. Retailers of clothing are usually happier at a distance from fast food takeaways or icecream kiosks for obvious reasons. Pedestrian flows are also improved by separating clothing shops from food shops because customers in the two shop clusters tend to shop at very different speeds. Supermarkets are best positioned with easy and, if possible, separate, access to the parking area. Other shop types, such as jewellers, hardware stores and record stores, seem suited to being scattered through the centre,

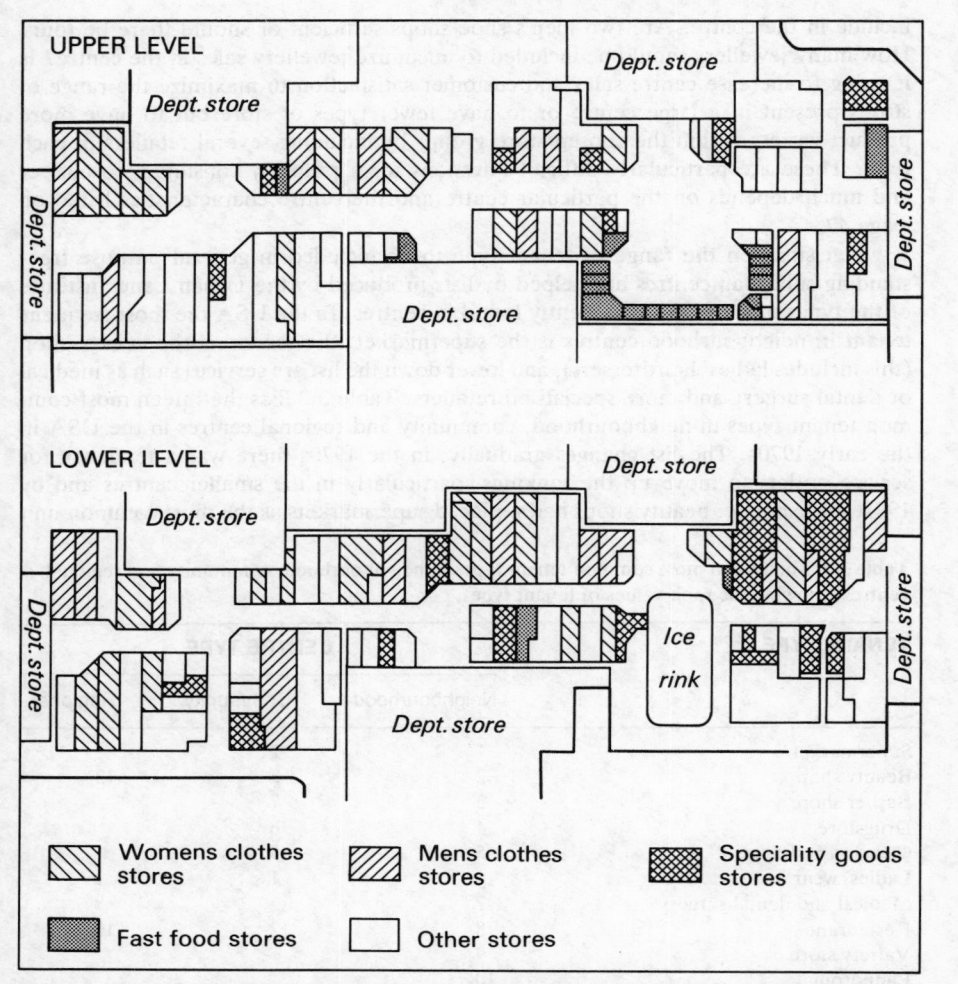

3.4 Location of selected store types within Prestonwood Regional centre in north Dallas, Texas

serving to sustain shopper interest. Figure 3.4 shows the location of selected store types in the Prestonwood Centre in north Dallas, Texas. In this super-regional centre there is a stringent tenant selection policy and a clear grouping of some tenant types, most noticeably the fast food services which are adjacent to the public ice rink which is integral to the centre.

The location of anchor tenants in the larger centres is an important aspect of tenant policy which impinges on the design of centre. Key tenants, as well as the centre as a whole, benefit from location at each end of a strip or mall rather than being placed together in the middle. Whilst centres can operate with a haphazard location of shop types within them, sales volumes can be increased considerably by an effective location component in tenant mix policy.

The third guideline in tenant mix is to obtain the correct range of tenants for the type of centre. It is also important to know how many tenants of a particular type to include in the centre. Are two men's shoe shops sufficient or should there be four? How many jewellers should be included to maximize jewellery sales in the centre? Is it going to increase centre sales and customer satisfaction to maximize the range of stores present in a large centre or to have fewer types of store but to have more product variety within the chosen store groups by including several retailers of each type? These are particularly difficult questions for a property consultant to answer and much depends on the particular centre and the centre characteristics listed on page 47.

Decisions on the range of tenant type to be included in general purpose free-standing suburban centres are helped by lists produced by the Urban Land Institute of the types of shop most frequently found in centres. In the USA the most frequent tenant in neighbourhood centres is the supermarket, the second is the beauty shop (this includes ladies' hairdressers), and lower down the list are services such as medical or dental surgery and more specialised retailers. Table 3.2 lists the fifteen most common tenant types in neighbourhood, community and regional centres in the USA in the early 1970s. The list changes gradually; in the 1970s there was a tendency for service outlets to move up the rankings, particularly in the smaller centres and by 1981, for example, beauty shops had replaced supermarkets as the most common unit

Table 3.2 The fifteen most common tenant types in neighbourhood, community and regional centres, showing the rank values of tenant types.

TENANT TYPE	CENTRE TYPE		
	Neighbourhood	Community	Regional
Supermarket	1	2	
Beauty shop	2	3	12
Barber shop	3	7	
Drugstore	4	6	
Cleaners and dyers	5	8	
Ladies' wear	6	1	1
Medical and dental surgery	7	5	8
Restaurant	8	12	10
Variety store	9		
Laundromat	10		
Bank	11	13	
Family shoe store	12	4	3
Garden/household goods	13	15	15
Off licence	14		
Estage Agency	15		
Men's wear		9	2
Junior department store		11	
Cards and gifts		14	5
Ladies' speciality/accessories			4
Ladies' shoe store			6
Jewellery		10	7
Confectioner			9
Department store			11
Music and records			13
Men's and boys' shoe store			14

Source: Urban Land Institute (1972)

in neighbourhood centres. Such lists form the basis of decisions on the range of shop type to be included in the centre but they do not help either with the question of the correct quantity of shops of one type or on tenant policies in other types of shopping centre. It is in the newer types of centre – focused centre, ancillary centre, renewal centre, etc. – where decisions on tenant mix policy are most difficult. In centres which are integrated into shopping districts such decisions are particularly hard as the shop range in the whole shopping district may have to be taken into consideration as an influence. The shop range in the shopping district can change rapidly and in an uncontrolled manner creating very considerable difficulties for the controlled tenant mix of the shopping centre. In focused shopping centres the product mix sold by the major tenant is a critical factor in determining the range of tenants in the subsidiary stores. A focused centre based on a hypermarket will probably have a tobacconist/ newsagent, fast food outlet, post office/bank/building society, ladies' clothing store, chemist/pharmacy, television rental, ladies' hairdresser and a butcher/baker/ greengrocer amongst the dozen or so smaller units. A centre based on a large DIY goods outlet, however, will have a quite different tenant range, probably including an estate agency, insurance agency, car parts retailer, furnishing store, fast food outlet, off licence and tobacconist/newsagent.

When the tenant mix plan is prepared at the preliminary planning phase of the centre development process, not only are there assessments to be made of the types of store to be included but also calculations of the rent and tenant control mechanisms. Clearly not all types of retailer can pay the same rent because of differences in profitability. In a discussion of tenant type, the Urban Land Institute, *Shopping Center Development Handbook* (1977) points out that:

> the developer must remember that all types of store cannot and should not pay the same rental per square foot . . . Certain types of service establishments may pay comparatively low rentals and may even be loss leaders for the center. Such tenants, however, are valuable to high rent tenants for their drawing power and for rounding out the centre's services to the community (p. 78).

Tenant control is necessary because having gone through the processes of creating a balanced tenant mix it would be potentially disastrous if a tenant radically changed trading method or product mix. The movement of a supermarket into non-food goods would affect the viability of other non-food retailers in a centre. In small strip centres where tenant mix plans have been less well formalized, such change does occur in an almost uncontrolled fashion and non-food retailers, for example, can suffer from changes in the product mix of the anchor supermarket. The problem moves from the retailer and becomes one for the centre developer/owner when the non-food retailer moves out and likely tenants see the range of goods on sale in the supermarket. One result in Britain has been the move of services – estate agents, building societies, etc. – into these small centres. Such problems show the need for a carefully thought out tenant plan at the planning stage and for the inclusion in the plan of mechanisms to control tenant trading behaviour.

This control, in large centres, is generally exercised through leases which define limits on the floorspace to be used to sell different types of goods. In Britain similar controls can be introduced through the land use planning system, such that development permission may be conditional on stores not exceeding certain limits on a food : non-food floorspace ratio. This control is used in permissions for focused shopping centres in Britain. Control through leases is widespread in the USA and Australia. The lease also controls the rent to be paid by the retailer and the structure of

Table 3.3 Estimate of first-year income for a hypothetical centre using fixed and percentage rent structure

TENANT	Floor area (m²)	RENTAL RATES				
		Square metre rate ($)	Percentage of sales rate	Minimum income ($)	Estimated sales ($)	Expected income ($)
Supermarket	1 950	15.0	1.25	31 700	2 400 000	31 700
Beauty shop	100	25.0	7	2 500	32 000	2 500
Barber shop	100	25.0	7	2 500	40 451	2 830
Shoe repair	50	25.0	7	1 200	14 000	1 200
Bakery	100	25.0	8	2 500	37 765	3 020
Drugstore	900	15.0	2.5	13 500	540 000	13 500
Ice Cream Parlor	75	30	8	2 250	250 000	2 250
Florist	75	25	8	1 875	28 732	2 010
Jewelry	50	25	6	1 250	20 665	1 250
Toy and hobby	150	25	6	3 750	64 048	3 840
Restaurant	200	25	6	5 000	97 584	5 850
Variety	500	17.5	5	8 750	157 500	8 750
Clothing & shoes	1 500	20	5	30 000	607 500	30 375
Hardware	396	20	5	7 920	140 000	7 920
Total	6 146			$114 445	$4 180 245	$117 495

the rent mechanism. Fixed rates per square metre with regular reviews used to be commonplace in large and small centres but increasingly *percentage rents* are being introduced certainly into large centres and in some of the newer centre types. Rents, in this case, consist of two parts, first a fixed rent per square metre and secondly an element related to sales volume which is triggered when a fixed sales level is reached. (The percentage rate and trigger point are not necessarily the same for all tenants.) Like income tax percentages, rentals can be applied on a sliding scale with several bands. Table 3.3 provides a hypothetical rent structure for the retail element of a typical neighbourhood centre in North America in the early 1970s. In this small centre the majority of estimated income comes from the fixed rents with percentage rents only being effective when the fixed rent is less than the percentage rent on total sales. Thus in the case of the supermarket no percentage rental is taken because 1.25 per cent of total sales is less than the fixed rent. The barber shop however pays a rent of 7 per cent of turnover made up of $2500 fixed rent and $330 percentage rent element.

The type of rental structure and the degree of lease control over the tenants affects the tenant mix and the way the centre changes after the initial development. Conflicts may arise over lease control with anchor tenants wanting to have a say in the tenant mix in the remainder of the centre. Smaller tenants may object to this influence by retailers rather than the developers and cases on this reached the courts in America during the 1970s. The Federal Trade Commission (FTC) has been involved several times and a case in Washington DC illustrates the issues:

> The specific complaint by the FTC states that the three anchor tenants of the mall had provisions within their leases which allowed them individually to approve or disapprove the leases of other tenants, allowed them to limit the floorspace allotted to other tenants . . . and allowed the three anchors to maintain control over how the other tenants do business in such areas as advertising and setting prices (Cooper, 1973, p. 1).

Lease clauses with this effect were not unusual in large centres not just in the USA but also in Canada, Australia and France (*Libre Service Actualité*, 1981) but as developers have become more established and less dependent on a few retail companies to anchor their schemes and government has questioned the legitimacy of such clauses, so there have been fewer of these restrictive lease arrangements. The annual survey of lease abstracts produced by *Chain Store Age* shows a decline in restrictive leases in the USA over the last twenty years. By creating a sound and fair tenant mix policy developers can avoid not only legal wrangling but also much of the conflict between anchor and other tenants which bedevilled some of the large developments of the 1960s. Solomon (1981) points out that 'flexibility and coordination' are the essential prerequisites to a good tenant plan.

The geographer looking at the mix of retail types present in a shopping centre is studying the results of conscious decisions and plans of the property consultant involved in the centre development. The final tenant mix plan drawn up is a basic document which influences both the financial success of the centre and the third major activity in the preliminary planning phase: centre design.

Design

The financial plan, the tenant mix plan and the design are closely interrelated and cannot be drawn up in isolation of each other. With the financial and tenant plans established, however, Gosling and Maitland (1976) in their study of large centre designs state that

The design problem . . . revolves around the manipulation of anchor stores, mall entry points, servicing arrangements and specialist shop distribution to achieve the greatest trading potential for the centre as a whole. The developer will have his own ideas as to the most advantageous distribution of particular shop types and the extent to which similar types should be grouped or dispersed. What emerges is a sort of chess game, with weightings given to individual pieces according to their draw, and rules governing the relationships between them. The architect's difficulty then lies in resolving this with the varying physical requirements of the pieces, with some requiring area but not frontage, and others the reverse. In practice this difficulty may well be overshadowed by the problem of establishing the rules themselves, for these spring directly from the number and nature of the anchor department stores, and should these factors change during the design stage then everything else must change with them (p. 29).

Whilst these points relate specifically to large centres the general principles are relevant to the creation of a design plan for any type of centre.

The keynote is directing the pedestrian flows into and within the centre to the social satisfaction of the pedestrian and to the economic satisfaction of the retailers, and so indirectly to the satisfaction of developers and financiers. Pedestrian and retailer requirements are not necessarily in conflict in this respect. Generally, the retail sales volume of a store is in direct proportion to the volume of pedestrian traffic passing the store entrance. Centre design therefore attempts to optimize pedestrian movement past shop frontages but in turn must not result in excessive customer movement (Koehler, 1973). Locating major anchor tenants at the ends of shopping malls and placing entrances from car parks on side malls are two design features that are widely used to manage pedestrian flow. Associated with this pedestrian management also is the provision of seating. Generally a ratio of between 1.0 and 1.8 seats per 100 m^2 GLA is used in most centres.

In the designs for larger centres, usually those of 10 000 m^2 and over, decisions have to be made on the number of levels in the centre and whether the centre is to be enclosed and fully air-conditioned or not. In the USA there has been a gradual change in the design of these large centres, from single-level open centres to single-level enclosed ones and most recently to multi-level enclosed centres. The more compact multi-level centres have proved to be no more expensive, as was once thought, than single-level structures and also they have the advantages of having fewer long stretches of uninterrupted pedestrian mall and higher efficiency levels in maintenance, energy use and infrastructure provision.

Different types of centre pose different design issues and consequently yield individual solutions. In speciality centres the theme may dictate the design, as in the Japan Centre in San Francisco. Similarly, centres in historic structures pose severe constraints on centre design (Gamzon, 1979; Schmertz, 1974).

The design plan extends to decisions on the whole site not just of the centre structure. Thus it includes parking plot layout and access and the amount of parking space necessary for the particular centre. The usual ratio applied is around 5.5 parking spaces per 100 m^2 GLA but again this may vary with particular circumstances. Ancillary centres do not require as many spaces whilst multi-purpose centres, which may have to provide employee or residential parking space in considerable numbers, may need more spaces per 100 m^2. The standard of 5.5 is usually applied to free-standing general prupose centres in North America but recent trends have been towards a reduction in the level of provision in newer centres to an index closer to 4.5. The car parking element of centre design is one of the few basic design features to differ widely in different countries.

The general building layouts discussed in the previous paragraphs are likely to be seen in Stockholm, Singapore or San Antonio. The essential design ingredient of the management of pedestrian movements is common to centres throughout the world. It is the associated features of the centre – car parking, servicing of the centre, public transport interchange provision, etc. – which differ so considerably from society to society. The high level of parking provision in many European hypermarket centres, sometimes as many as ten spaces per 100 m^2, contrasts with the very low levels of such provision in most types of centre in the Third World. The integration of public transport interchanges into centres is common in renewal centres in Britain as it is in the larger centres in Japan. Broad social differences will result in contrasting design plans but the influence of land use planners considering the community benefits of the centre is also considerable in determining the presence or absence of social functions in the centre.

Increasingly in the design plan it is necessary to explore the likely environmental impact of the proposed centre. In many countries there is an obligation on potential developers to assess impacts both on the natural and on the economic environment and to incorporate design features to minimize socially undesirable impact. For instance, new centres are more heavily landscaped than the concrete block centres of the 1960s. The economic effects of new centres on existing retail investments are also forecast and new centres adapted to reduce the more disastrous aspects of such forecasts. Government agencies are usually involved in the centre development process at this stage and their role will be considered more fully in Chapters 5 and 6.

During the preliminary planning stage, the finance, tenant and design plans are evolving continuously with changes in one affecting the others. The developer is at the centre of this process and, by the time of its completion, should be able to visualize the final centre form. This stage is usually the longest, and most complex and critical of the entire process. During this stage decisions are made which will affect the social and commercial success of the development.

The final planning stage

The third stage of the planning phase is one of final planning when earlier plans are refined and contracts prepared. It is likely that at this stage a detailed estimate of the overall costs and revenues of the project will be made and the final decision taken on whether or not to proceed. Examples of the coordination of finance, tenant and design plans into the final plan for centre development are given in a study by Applebaum (1970) of a regional centre scheme, whilst the case studies in Applebaum and Kaylin (1974) provide details of a finance plan and its evaluation, the working out of a tenant plan, and more comprehensive plans incorporating financial, tenant mix and design considerations. It is relatively unusual for the development process to have reached the final plan stage and then be cancelled, though the final construction stage may be delayed by adverse prevailing economic conditions such as abnormally high interest rates.

THE CONSTRUCTION PHASE

The second main phase of the development process is that of construction. The engineers and construction companies take over and put into operation the plans of earlier stages. There is considerable variability in the degree to which the developer is involved in the actual shop-fitting activities at the end of construction. In the USA it is common for the construction phase to be undertaken in its entirety by a single organization, whilst elsewhere it is more common for only the construction of the shell to take place and then for individual tenants to arrange their own shop design and building. The construction phase activities generally fall outside the sphere of interest and expertise of geographers – unless they happen to be earning a little extra money as construction workers!

THE OPENING PHASE

The final phase of the development process is the opening and continuing management of the centre. Opening events can vary from a simple 'Open for Business' sign to ceremonial tape-cutting by royalty. The effect of new centre openings on the established pattern of centre provision has been widely studied for many types of centre (Smith and Kelley, 1960; Fry, 1961; Walker, 1957; Lewison and Showalter, 1977; Frazier, 1974; Bennison and Davies, 1980; *Real Estate Analyst*, 1970). The incorporation of the new centre into the network of centres takes place, in a strict sense, after the development process has been completed. Centre developers are obviously interested in the continued health of the centre and its constituent retailers but the monitoring of centre use and operation falls beyond the scope of this chapter.

This chapter has shown the shopping centre development process to be complex but one in which there is a sequence of activities common to all types of centre in all societies. In order to carry out development a group of specialist professions has emerged over the last forty years. Of these the centre developer acts as the catalyst, provides the initial idea and coordinates the process. The role of the developer is, 'to make the new centre happen; to assemble the finance, land, tenants and professional and building skills in such a way that a complete shopping centre would be produced by a certain date and thereafter function in such a way as to provide a satisfactory return on the capital invested' (Gosling and Maitland, 1976, p. 28). With the growth of the shopping centre industry, shopping centre developers have become potent forces shaping urban landscapes and influencing the daily lives of many hundreds of millions of consumers. To understand the spatial patterns and processes of centre provision it is necessary to appreciate the complexity of the development process within which location is but one of many considerations. Location is the one factor with which geographers have become most involved in recent decades; it is probably the single most important factor determining the success of a given centre; it is the part of centre development over which government agencies, particularly land use planners, have most influence; and it is the subject of the next chapter.

CHAPTER 4
SHOPPING CENTRE LOCATION

The selection of a suitable site comes early in the centre development process. Potential locations are assessed in terms of their commerical viability. This assessment includes consideration of the potential market at regional and local level and also involves evaluation of the land use planning and other governmental controls likely to affect proposed sites. Different factors of location operate depending on the scale being considered. *Inter-regional* patterns of location are determined, for the main part, by three factors: first, by national patterns of regional economic growth; secondly, by government particularly through policies of new settlement planning; and thirdly, by regional differentials in site and construction costs. Within regions, at the *inter-urban* scale, centre location patterns are related first to city size, and for some centre types to a hierarchial diffusion process, and secondly to the effects of local entrepreneurial activity. Within a city or town, at the *intra-urban* level, the location pattern of shopping centres is influenced by land use planning policy and philosophy, the general suburbanization process and market area economics. The purpose of this chapter is to review locational patterns at each of these three scales. Chapters 5 and 6 will focus on specific centre types.

INTER-REGIONAL PATTERNS IN THE USA

Regional patterns of population change may be seen as a major factor in recent shifts in the pattern of centre development in the USA. Centre development in the 1950s focused on the traditional regions of economic wealth in the north-east and California. Figure 4.1, from Cohen's (1972) study of regional centre diffusion, shows that cities where the first centre was developed before 1958 are strongly concentrated in the traditional industrial belt. The economic expansion of the southern states brought in its wake shopping centre development and Cohen's map shows how initial penetration of southern cities by large centres took place in the 1960s. In the 1960s and 1970s the shift of economic power from the north-east to southern and western cities, the *sun-belt cities*, has been a consistent feature of the American space economy. Whilst Figure 4.1 shows initial locations of major shopping centres, the general centre of gravity of all shopping centre development has moved to the south. The rapid population and economic growth in southern California in the 1960s and in Texas, Florida and Georgia in the 1970s resulted in cities in these states becoming places of intense expansion of the shopping centre industry.

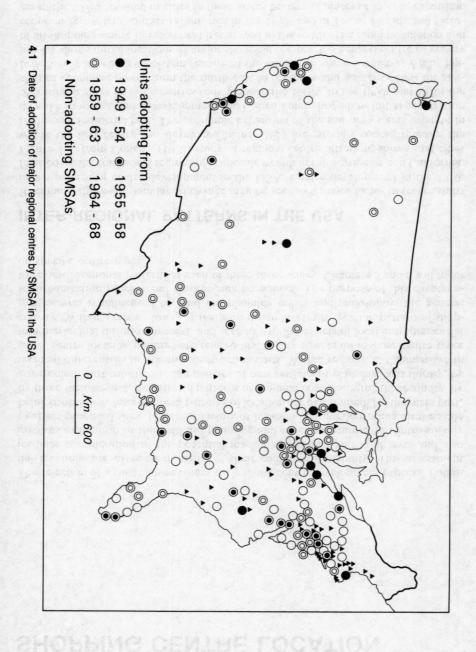

4.1 Date of adoption of major regional centres by SMSA in the USA

Units adopting from

● 1949 - 54   ◉ 1955 - 58

◎ 1959 - 63   ○ 1964 - 68

▸ Non-adopting SMSAs

0   Km   600

Development opportunities in the southern states have been considerable because of the lack of earlier development and the present population growth and also for negative reasons associated with the north-eastern states where competition from established centres is strong and population numbers are stabilizing. It is nevertheless a pattern of differential growth, not one of southern growth as against northern decline. Table 4.1, using data from the biennial surveys by *Shopping Center World*, shows the growth in shopping centres, of 929 m² and larger, in those states with 500 or more centres in 1981. The three states with the most centres in 1981 were California, Texas and Florida and together they accounted for over 27 per cent of the centres in the USA. In the early 1970s Florida displaced New York as the third ranking state in this table. Although directly comparable data are not available for the 1960s the available data indicate that Ohio was one of the top four states at that time. Of the states shown in Table 4.1 comparison of the state and national rates of growth of centre numbers during the 1970s shows Texas, Florida and Georgia to be states of rapid growth together with North Carolina, Missouri and Pennsylvania. Pennsylvania appears anomalous but 1974 marked the end year of the period of rapid growth. By the end of that year, 685 centres were in operation and the growth rate for the second half of the decade is much more comparable to that of other north-eastern states. In these north-eastern states, however, growth was certainly occurring in the 1970s; only one state, Ohio, did not increase floorspace by 50 per cent between 1973 and 1981. It must be remembered moreover, that these floorspace increases of 50 per cent and over are related to already large floorspace figures. It is the same with shopping centre sales: the comparatively low growth figures for New York, Massachusetts and Ohio are low only by comparison with the rocket-like growth in Texas or Missouri. Whilst much has been written about the regional shifts in economic

Table 4.1 Development of shopping centres of 929 m² or more between 1973 and 1981 in the USA in states with more than 500 centres on 1 January 1981

STATES	NUMBER OF CENTRES		% CHANGE 1973–81		
	1.1.1973	1.1.1981	Number of centres	Floorspace	Sales*
California	1 739	2 813	61.8	61.9	178.7
Texas	1 077	1 902	76.6	103.6	263.4
Florida	700	1 317	88.1	97.1	242.8
New York	696	967	38.9	54.4	167.8
Pennsylvania	450	884	96.4	91.1	257.6
Ohio	590	838	42.0	45.9	158.4
Georgia	373	765	105.1	100.9	249.2
Missouri	300	755	151.6	137.2	281.9
Illinois	471	747	58.5	93.9	247.7
Massachusetts	423	641	51.5	50.8	151.7
North Carolina	329	589	79.0	98.1	237.5
Virginia	373	551	47.7	64.2	179.5
Michigan	324	526	62.3	74.7	258.1
Indiana	352	521	48.0	56.6	188.2
USA	13 174	22 050	67.3	79.6	213.0

* Sales refer to year totals for 1972 and 1980
Source: Shopping Centre World (1973, 1981c)

Table 4.2 Proportion of total USA centre development activity, 1973–81, accounted for by the top ten growth states 1981

STATES	% OF CENTRES		% OF FLOORSPACE		% OF SALES	
	1973	1981	1973	1981	1973	1981
California	13.20	12.75	12.66	11.42	12.43	11.07
Texas	8.17	8.63	7.15	8.52	6.53	7.58
Florida	5.31	5.97	5.67	6.22	5.60	6.13
New York	5.28	4.38	6.03	5.19	6.50	5.56
Pennsylvania	3.41	4.01	4.72	5.02	4.69	5.35
Ohio	4.47	3.80	6.04	4.91	6.30	5.21
Georgia	2.83	3.47	2.41	2.70	2.42	2.70
Missouri	2.27	3.42	2.21	2.91	2.29	2.79
Illinois	3.57	3.39	3.84	4.15	3.99	4.44
Massachusetts	3.21	2.91	3.07	2.58	3.47	2.79
TOTAL	51.72	52.73	54.16	53.62	54.22	53.62

power in the USA and absolute economic decline of the north-east, there is so far little evidence of absolute decline in the shopping centre industry. Certainly growth rates are lower than in the south and west but limited growth is still occurring in the north-east.

Disaggregation of the data by centre type would show little recent development of traditional suburban free-standing centres in the larger north-eastern cities but a notable increase in development activity in respect of downtown and speciality centres. Much of the southern city growth remains in general purpose traditional centre development (see Ch. 5).

Table 4.2 shows the degree of concentration of shopping centre development in the top ten states of 1981. As might be expected the state share of national totals increased sharply in southern states and declined in the north-east. California's dominance declined notably during the 1970s with centre expansion slackening due to the existing high levels of competition. Well over half the shopping centres in the USA are located in only ten states, either in the traditional manufacturing belt or the rapidly growing sunbelt. Some insights into the relationship between these dominant states and other parts of the USA may be gained by a simple shift-share analysis.

Shift-share analysis of floorspace totals

By applying standard shift-share analysis (Stilwell, 1968) to floorspace data by size of centre for each state, it is possible to disaggregate centre floorspace growth in a given period into three components:

1 A national share component which is the amount floorspace would have increased during the period under consideration if regional floorspace had increased at the same rate as for the whole of the USA. This component measures national growth and response to such national factors as interest rates.
2 A composition shift component which is the extra amount by which floorspace in the region has increased as a result of the region having a particular size distribution of centres. Different sizes of centre have increased at different national rates and this shift is positive if the region has above average representation of centres in nationally fast-growing size classes and negative for regions with a high proportion of floorspace in centres in slower growing size classes. This component reflects the

structural changes taking place in the centre industry with, for example, the growth of super-regional centres.

3 A differential shift component which reflects the growth performance of each size class of centre compared with national rates for each size class. This shift will be positive if floorspace increased more than would be expected given the size distribution of centres, whilst a negative value indicates floorspace increased less than might be expected from the size mix of centres existing at the start of the period. This component is considered as representing the local business climate and the regional element in shopping centre floorspace growth.

From the earlier discussion of regional changes in the USA it might be anticipated that, in a shift-share analysis of recent years, there would be large positive differential shifts in the growth states such as Texas, Florida and Georgia and negative differential shifts in the north-east. The earlier growth in the north-east and California, however, will have laid the foundations of the size distribution of centres and so these states are likely to have a high representation of the faster growing size classes and hence a positive composition shift unlike southern states where growth, until recently, was slower than in the north. Furthermore given the spatial structure of the shopping centre industry and its dynamic nature, then the national share component may be expected to constitute a large element in the total growth of floorspace. Finally amongst the states with relatively low levels of centre investment we might expect the growth pattern to become increasingly similar to the national pattern as development occurs.

Table 4.3 shows the shift-share components for selected states in respect of floorspace change in three periods in the second half of the 1970s. The data again are

Table 4.3 Shift-share components of floorspace ('000 m²) change in selected states in the USA, 1975–81

STATE	1975–77			1977–79			1979–81		
	NS	CS	DS	NS	CS	DS	NS	CS	DS
Arizona	688	3	686	426	696	−205	858	−18	−85
California	4701	166	−1450	2301	220	88	4900	135	−3
Delaware	185	−31	−24	91	−16	−27	184	16	−40
Florida	2325	−119	256	1227	−84	76	2581	15	621
Georgia	1066	−79	97	558	3	−146	1147	−29	129
Illinois	1558	253	955	930	163	−510	1894	134	−821
Kentucky	527	−32	−208	251	−39	122	545	−31	120
Massachusetts	1200	−103	−554	491	−67	765	1163	−41	−299
New Jersey	1296	128	−776	614	50	−254	1254	37	−947
New York	2225	246	202	1205	148	−696	2434	104	−1375
North Dakota	74	−12	−30	34	−6	93	89	15	51
Ohio	2236	23	−1078	1065	−18	−846	2081	75	129
Pennsylvania	2052	50	−412	973	12	−26	2044	57	705
South Dakota	39	−5	59	25	−3	117	75	−4	16
Texas	2952	−56	1431	1652	−29	401	3545	−60	863
Vermont	59	17	25	32	6	98	85	10	18
Virginia	1220	−67	−398	592	−56	−121	1212	−36	−582

Notes: NS is the national share component
CS is the composition shift component
DS is the differential shift component

Table 4.4 Percentage change in floorspace (GLA) by size of centre in USA, 1973–81

CENTRE SIZE (m²)	1973–75	1975–77	1977–79	1979–81
929–9290	15.6	21.4	9.0	12.8
9291–18 580	9.4	20.4	8.1	18.9
18 581–37 160	12.2	20.1	6.3	16.5
37 161–74 320	10.0	19.8	8.2	20.7
over 74 320	23.6	70.3	27.1	28.0
All centres	13.6	24.8	9.7	18.8

drawn from the biennial census of centres provided in *Shopping Center World*. The six size classes of centre considered are shown in Table 4.4 which also shows the national rates of change for the different centre sizes in the three periods.

Table 4.3 shows the importance of the national share component in several states and, as might be expected, it is most important in those states shown in Tables 4.1 and 4.2 as being the foci of past development activity. Large differential shifts are apparent for Texas and Florida but less so for Georgia where the structure of growth appears closely related to the national average. Negative differential components occur for New York, Illinois, Massachusetts and several other northern states. In some cases these have appeared very recently, even within this period of change since 1975. But these states show the expected positive composition shift, suggesting a better than average representation of faster growing centre sizes in their centre size distribution. The states of Pennsylvania and Ohio are interesting for the most recent period here shows a positive differential shift which may reflect the emergence of new types of centre in these two states which have been the traditional locations for innovation in the shopping centre industry. Certainly in both states several downtown redevelopment centres have become operational since 1979. Amongst the smaller states such as Arizona, South Dakota and Vermont the figures become complicated because single large centre projects in each state result in a major increase in the state's total floorspace but, in many cases, in these smaller states the growth patterns have tended towards the national one. The national trend to the development of smaller centres compared with large centres, as seen the Table 4.4, has encouraged developers to look at smaller markets in states with less centre activity and to build up the floorspace in small and medium sized centres in these states thus bringing them closer to the national average. General development costs tend to be lower in these 'middle markets' where there is less competition for available sites both from other users and within the centre development industry.

Several trends in the inter-regional pattern of centre development are apparent in the USA. First, there is the rapid development of large traditional centres in the states with rapid economic growth. Secondly, there is a relative decline in activity in states with a longer established centre tradition. Thirdly, there is the development of the new centre types particularly in states with an already well established, but slower growing, centre industry. Finally, there is a trend towards growth in activity in smaller centres in middle markets, notably in those states with relatively few existing centres. Within this pattern the influence of inter-regional trends in general economic growth is the major determinant of the three factors influencing inter-regional centre development. The factors of government and development cost differentials give the detailed background to the general picture of centre location.

INTER-REGIONAL PATTERNS IN THE UNITED KINGDOM AND FRANCE

In the UK, government intervention and inter-regional site cost differentials are the most important of the three major factors. The different attitudes planners in different authorities adopt to development applications can result in different levels of centre activity in the local government areas (see Ch. 6). This is particularly the case with controversial types of centre such as those focused on a hypermarket. These differentials are relevant mainly at the inter-urban scale because the area of control of individual planning authorities is relatively small. Table 4.5 based on work by Schiller and Lambert (1977), however, does show broad regional differences in the extent of central area redevelopment schemes in England and Wales. The relative lack of schemes in Greater London can be explained by the difference in the land use planning machinery compared with that in the rest of the country and also by the greater difficulty, and hence higher costs, in acquiring sites in densely developed centres with highly fragmented ownership patterns as is the case in the suburban shopping districts in the London region. A general planning strategy for Greater London was not finally agreed until the early 1970s and it was not until after this plan was implemented that developers and land use planners could actively and effectively prepare proposals for large shopping centres (see Ch. 6). The difficulties of site acquisition also held back development so that by 1977, the date of the Schillier and Lambert survey, relatively few centres were either operational or firmly planned. In the subsequent four years, however, the position changed drastically and by 1981 almost all the major shopping districts in suburban London have either plans for a central area redevelopment centre or have one already trading. So large centre development was held back in a region which might, in purely economic terms, have been expected to be in the vanguard of British centre development.

Conversely in France the Paris plan of 1960 encouraged polycentric metropolitan development in which large shopping centres were to play a vital and catalytic role. The earlier date of the agreed plan in Paris than in London allowed planners and centre developers to work together at the innovation phase of the modern French shopping centre development. The economic growth of the Paris region coupled with positive governmental encouragement of shopping centres allowed site acquisition

Table 4.5 Proportion of large town centres in England and Wales with a central city shopping centre of at least 4645 m² in use or under construction in 1977

REGION	TOWNS WITH CENTRAL AREA SALES OVER £10 MILLION IN 1977		
	With scheme	% with scheme	without scheme
Yorkshire and North-East	16	73	6
North-West and North Wales	21	88	3
Midlands and East Anglia	23	72	9
South Wales and South-West	9	60	6
London	10	34	19
Rest of South-East	26	79	7
TOTAL	105	68	50

Source: Schiller and Lambert (1977)

Table 4.6 Shopping centres in France with over 40 000 m² floorspace in operation 1980

CENTRE	CITY REGION	FLOORSPACE (m²)	LOCATION*
Créteil-Soleil	Paris	96 180	C
Rosny 2	Paris	95 120	P
Part Dieu	Lyon	92 000	C
Vélizy 2	Paris	88 500	P
Belle-Epine	Paris	86 900	P
Parinor	Paris	73 500	P
Evry	Paris	68 000	C
Cap 3000	Nice	62 000	P
Les Flanades	Paris	61 000	P
Barnéoud	Marseille	59 000	P
Parly 2	Paris	58 275	P
Trois Fontaines	Paris	52 870	P
Partet S/Garonne	Toulouse	52 000	P
Galaxie	Paris	52 000	C
Ulis 2	Paris	51 640	P
Ile Napoléon	Mulhouse	48 000	P
Grand Var	Toulon	46 000	P
Marseille-Bourse	Marseille	46 000	C
Englos-Auchan	Lille	45 000	C
Grand Place	Grenoble	43 500	C
Alma	Rennes	43 000	C
Barentin	Rouen	40 770	C
St Maximin	Paris	40 000	C
Forum	Paris	40 000	C

*Note: P = peripheral;   C = town centre within city region

problems to be overcome easily and not to generate major site cost differentials between Paris and other regions. Large shopping centre development therefore focused on the Paris region and only since the mid-1970s have schemes of over 40 000 m² become commonplace in other economically strong regions. Table 4.6 lists the centres of 40 000 m² and over in operation in early 1980 and the dominance of the Paris region is clearly apparent.

Amongst the smaller centres, many of which are focused centres based on hypermarkets, regional development patterns have been responses to general economic differentials. Strong expansion has occurred in the Paris region and in the growth regions in the south, for example those based on Marseille and Toulouse. The governmental decision in June 1981 to suspending all authorizations for new centre developments involving a large store has placed a total halt on the development process. The ultimate result of this policy may well be a considered national plan of centre development in which inter-regional locational patterns will be controlled by economic planners within a central government agency (see Ch. 6).

The three determinants of the inter-urban pattern of centre development have been outlined in the differing contexts of the USA, UK and France. These examples show how the three factors – general economic trends, government and development cost differentials – have differing relative importance in determining the regional pattern of shopping centres.

INTER-URBAN PATTERNS OF DEVELOPMENT

The differentials amongst regions in their degree of shopping centre development provide the background to the differentials produced by variations in city size, the presence or absence of local shopping centre entrepreneurs and the differences in policy amongst land use planning authorities.

Cohen's (1972) study of major centres in North America showed how the larger cities generally were the earliest group to play host to centre developers. Table 4.6 shows that the same is apparently true for the larger centres in France and is not an unexpected feature of large centre development. In Australia large centre development is notably concentrated in state capitals which comprise the larger cities. In the Third World the same is true again. Large centres appear first in the large cities and also it is in these cities that the subsequent concentration of large centre activity takes place. With the medium sized centres, typically less than 30 000 m², the inter-urban patterns in all types of country, and in both initial penetration and subsequent development, are much more complex. Undoubtedly there is a city size variable involved with, for example, central area extension centre, infill centres, even neighbourhood and strip centres, all more likely to be developed first in larger towns rather than smaller ones. There are many exceptions to such a general pattern but, before these exceptions are explored, it is useful to consider briefly the general process related to city size.

The development opportunities in larger cities are initially wide-ranging and extensive. As development occurs the range of acceptable undeveloped locations is reduced directly, and indirectly, by reducing the development potential of sites close to those which are developed. There comes a point, therefore, where the range of undeveloped opportunities provided by a smaller city is larger than that remaining in the larger city. This clearly occurs long before market saturation is reached in the larger city. Such a simple model is obviously complicated by many factors such as urban growth and the competitive tactics practised by existing centres but at a rather simple level it does account, in part, for the trend towards middle market projects not only in North America but also in Europe and Australia. Opsata (1980), commenting on the general review of scale economy arguments underway in North America, suggests that 'There is considerable evidence that development is beginning to move into smaller areas that would have been ignored a few years ago . . . When shopping centres were new phenomena in this country, site selection was unhampered by market saturation or existing competition' (p. 29). The emerging interest in middle markets has resulted in the development of fully enclosed, free-standing general purpose centres of community-level size but fulfilling a regional function and with a tenant mix more like a regional centre. The store size is generally smaller with the department store units from 6000 m² to 10 000 m², or about half the size usually associated with a full regional centre. These centres are cheaper and quicker to build than full regional centres (Peterson, 1976). Middle markets are usually considered as cities with 50 000–100 000 population in the urban and trade areas and a centre of 20 000 m²–25 000 m² can operate effectively as the single dominant centre in the city (Muller, 1978). In the USA considerable development of these centres in middle sized towns is currently underway in several states in the Great Plains region. Some developers are specializing, very successfully, in this type of centre; CBL & Associates based in Chattanooga (Dunham, 1981) and Ainbinder Associates based in Houston, recently merged with the Canadian developer, Bramlea of Toronto in 1982, are typical of these smaller but rapidly growing development companies. Ainbinder

Associates opened ten new centres in 1980, all in middle markets, with an average GLA of just under 20 000 m² per centre, in towns in Oklahoma, Texas, North Dakota, South Dakota, Colarado and New Mexico. The presence of one of these 'mini-malls' in a town may act as a stimulus for general urban development in that town, at the expense of other competing cities. The activity in middle markets in the USA results in notable inter-urban differentials in centre development and shows the working of a development process related to city size.

A second feature of the relationship of city size to centre development is apparent in several European Countries and in Australia. This is the development of focused shopping centres again in the middle markets. In France these focused centres are usually based on a hypermarket, a pattern which emerged in the late 1960s. In Australia the Woolworth Company has designed a standard centre based on a combination of a large supermarket and a discount department store which together function in much the same way as the European hypermarket. These focused centres tend to be smaller than the American mini-malls, usually between 12 000 m² and 18 000 m², but they are very much a feature of medium sized towns where they dominate retail provision. The larger country towns in New South Wales have played host to these schemes since the mid-1970s with centres often based on a Woolco store and developed by this large retail group. The potential for investment in middle markets has also been realised in Britain where Jones Lang Wootton (1978), in a study of the location factor affecting investment in shops and, by implication, shopping centres, suggest that 'The best potential for rental growth is probably in those towns in the shopping hierarchy which are tending to graduate from market town' [defined as having a catchment population between 50 000 and 100 000] to sub-regional status . . . [because] the fastest rate of retail growth between 1961 and 1971 is shown in the sub-regional and market town centres' (p. 4).

City size relationships, however, are only one of several determinants of the inter-urban locational pattern of shopping centres. Attitudes of local land use planning agencies can be critical in affecting inter-urban patterns, particularly in the UK. The requirement on local planning authorities to prepare a town plan showing how the town land use pattern should evolve can be a catalyst to shopping centre development of many types, but it can also serve to warn developers that there is little chance of them obtaining permissions for development. Further, planning authorities in different towns can have contrasting approaches to central area redevelopment shopping centres; one authority may encourage renovation of the existing shops in the central shopping district whilst another may choose to promote various types of redevelopment centre.

In the city of Derby (population approximately 210 000), for example, the town plan positively encouraged shopping centre development. This policy has resulted in the central area of the city having a large core replacement scheme of 34 700 m², several extension centres together totalling over 10 000 m², a number of small infill centres of around 1500 m² and a speciality centre of 706 m² of retail space and 800 m² of offices in the refurbished Corn Exchange building which dates from 1862. The conscious policy in Derby of consolidating and concentrating major shopping centre development in the central area is typical of many British cities. Alongside the central city schemes, however, such authorities with a positive view of shopping centre activity also often allow neighbourhood and strip centre development in residential suburbia. So for example in Derby large housing estates built by the city housing department are served by small strip centres developed by the housing authority. Small neighbourhood centres have been provided in suburban residential estates built since the

1960s. The provision of small suburban centres is effectively an integral part of the general retail plan for the city and this plan has encouraged the building of shopping centres. In other cities, sometimes much larger, as for example Sheffield, the aim of planning policy in the central shopping district has been renovation and rebuilding of individual units and the pedestrianization of the central area rather than shopping centre development. Shopping centre development, however, has been encouraged in suburban areas through designation of sites for neighbourhood centres and focused centres. The overall level of centre development activity however is much lower in such cities than in cities with a policy, and town plan, which encourage shopping centre investment. While these examples of the influence of planning policy have been drawn from Britain, similar inter-urban distinctions occur in any country with effective land use planning legislation which is implemented at the local level. The effects of land use policy in the USA, UK and France in controlling specific types of shopping centre are explored in more detail in Chapters 5 and 6.

A third important variable in inter-urban patterns is the presence or absence in a city of entrepreneurs, particularly centre developers. Although many centres are planned and developed by organizations with a nationwide or even international sphere of operation the presence of local entrepreneurs is nevertheless important both in the early stages of centre development in a country and in the development of the smaller, less traditional types of centre. Mention was made in Chapter 1 of the con-. centration of centre building in Ohio in the 1950s where several centre developers, who ultimately grew to national organisations, were based in the state and carried out early development in cities in the state which were familiar to them. The Don Casto organization based in Columbus, Ohio, developed between 1951 and 1956 six centres in suburban Columbus. In Britain the same phenomenon can be seen with the early development of Arndale centres in towns in Yorkshire where the development company initially was based. In the early stages of growth of the shopping centre industry in a country the presence of entrepreneurs in a city or region may result in distinct inter-urban differentials in patterns of shopping centre location.

Even where there is an established industry, small centres tend still to be developed by local entrepreneurs, either by local centre developers or by local retail chains. In Perth, Western Australia, for example, a considerable impetus to suburban shopping centre development has been provided by a single retail chain, Boans, who have had a conscious corporate policy of centre investment and as a result had, in the early 1970s, a junior department store in many of the community-level centres in the city. This active involvement also so encouraged centre development that, for its population at the time, Perth had more shopping centre floorspace than any other Australian city. The presence of an active group of local entrepreneurs was not the only reason for the large quantity of floorspace but it was a significant factor in the establishment of a strong shopping centre industry in the city.

INTRA-URBAN PATTERNS OF CENTRE LOCATION

Within cities there are notably different patterns of centre location. Comparison of Figures 2.1 and 2.2 of the pattern of provision in San Antonio and Canberra shows in the one case a locational pattern which is a response to social and income differentials in the urban population and in the other the effect of a rigidly-implemented land use plan. Both patterns show the effects of strong pressures for the suburbanization of retail activity but it is useful to distinguish between patterns within established cities and the pattern of shopping centres created in new towns where retail and residential development have been phased together.

According to location theory, assuming the unconstrained entry of centres into an established city we would expect, as in the classic ice cream salesman problem, centres to locate adjacent to each other. This is indeed the case in many cities in the USA, for example in San Antonio where, at the intersection of the main Loop 410 with Highway 281 (a major arterial road to the northern suburbs), two quadrants of the intersection are filled with two large regional shopping centres. North Star Mall was developed in 1960 by the Rouse Company as a 50 000 m² GLA enclosed centre with two large department stores and 85 other units. In 1968 Central Park Mall of about the same size and with 78 units, also including two department stores, was opened adjacent to North Star Mall. Central Park was developed in close association with Sears, Roebuck, the department store chain, and was financed by a large government employees' life insurance company. Intense competition obviously resulted and the centres have trade areas with considerable overlap. By 1980 after a decade of competition North Star Mall began a major renovation and extension project, one aim of which was to provide more small units with higher rent/m² and which would add more variety to the tenant mix. Also after twenty years of operation general redesign and renovation was necessary (see Ch. 5) in order to compete with the slightly newer adjacent Central Park Mall. An interesting point about both malls is that they are relatively close to San Antonio airport and well placed to attract the custom of wealthy Mexicans who fly to San Antonio on shopping trips. Tenant mix in the centres reflects the demands of this type of customer; North Star Mall in particular seeks positively to attract them by advertising in Mexican newspapers. This search for international consumers is partly in response to the competition between two centres at effectively the same location. By adjacent location the two centres benefit from consumers visiting both centres on a single trip.

Such adjacent locations for similar types of centre is not unusual in large metropolitan areas in the USA. Not only regional and super-regional centres are involved, as in San Antonio, but it is also commonplace for community or neighbourhood centres to group around a key suburban intersection. This is particularly the case in higher-income suburban areas where, as was pointed out previously, centre development is most intense. All four quadrants of land at key intersections in the residential road network may be developed with neighbourhood type centres. Each is in competition with the other but each also benefits from the presence of the others in producing a shopping district which is larger and more attractive than any of the individual constituent centres. Whilst principles of trade area optimization underpin the development of similar centres on adjacent sites there are also economies of agglomeration to be obtained.

From the retailers' point of view agglomeration economies are a major aspect in deciding to locate in a centre but advantages inherent in grouped locations also exist for the shopping centres themselves. This is particularly the case for smaller centres close to major centres. Strip centres and even speciality centres, for example those specializing in motor accessory products, benefit from auxiliary locations adjacent to larger centres (Mason and Moore, 1972; Opsata, 1979). The smaller centre effectively enlarges its trade area by operating next to a large centre. This relationship has analogies with epiphytic processes in plant communities whilst the adjacent location of similar size centres places them in a symbiotic relationship. The location of such points of agglomeration within the city is the result of considerations of potential consumer spending, and accessibility. Usually such locations are suburban but when once developed, then consideration may be given to slightly less advantageous sites and different centre types such as redevelopment in central city sites and shopping centre building in lower income areas.

Although some features of this hypothetical and unconstrained intra-urban pattern are seen in cities in the USA the urban land use planning mechanism impinges on the development process. The zoning system in the USA exaggerates the importance of accessibility and agglomeration processes in the suburbs by its frequent designation of land adjacent to major road intersections for commercial uses. By zoning for commercial use land adjacent to intersections in suburban areas which are not yet developed but where growth is expected, the zoning mechanism can serve to concentrate new centre investment to create locations for the catalytic type centres mentioned previously (Ch. 1). Other types of land use planning can enhance the attractiveness of downtown locations for redevelopment centres and for the development of the newer types of more specialist shopping centre.

In contrast to this essentially North American pattern of intra-urban location, in Britain the land use planning machinery has lessened agglomeration considerations in suburban residential areas and has enhanced accessibility considerations in central area locations. The development plan and structure plan mechanisms of comprehensive land use planning operating since 1947 effectively predetermine, for new suburban areas, the appropriate floorspace provision for a particular location and then a single centre is developed. The location of the centre is also decided by the plan makers and is determined by reference to the perceived needs of the community. The planner, sometimes with the aid of public participation, decides on broadly how much centre floorspace is to be developed and where it will be located. An integral part of this decision making is an examination of the accessibility of alternative sites. Only in the case of renewal centres within an established shopping district is there the opportunity for developers and retailers to benefit from agglomeration economies and in such cases the general location is predetermined by prior developments. Even in central areas the opportunity for symbiotic and epiphytic locations is limited severely by site availability but certainly there are advantages, for example in an infill centre being adjacent to a core replacement scheme, or in an extension centre adjoining a large multi-use centre. In many British cities a core replacement scheme has had the effect of stimulating other types of centre development in adjacent locations. In Central Manchester, for example, a major core replacement scheme, the Arndale Centre of over 90 000 m^2, stimulated the creation of the Royal Exchange Centre – a speciality centre of forty-one small units on three levels in an historic building – both by its adjacent location and by the fact that the previous major tenant of the Royal Exchange Building moved into the Arndale Centre. Although planning permissions have to be granted by land use planners for renewal centres within a shopping district, the land use planning machinery, other than for large core replacement centres, tends not to be able to promote centre development in the positive way it can in new suburban areas.

LOCATIONS IN COMPREHENSIVELY-PLANNED CITIES

Within New Towns not only is the centre development of the suburbs carefully managed by land use planners but they are also able to promote centre development within the central area. Thus in Figure 2.1 of the centres in Canberra the regular distribution of centres in the suburbs is complemented by a group of centres, of different types, which constitute the city centre shopping district. Both the quantity and location of shopping centre floorspace is carefully planned and developers are required to work within this predetermined locational framework. In some New Town schemes, the city centre is a single centre as in most British New Towns. In others, as in Canberra, it comprises a group of interacting shopping centres. In either case the amount of floorspace is controlled and is part of a general retail plan for the New Town. Such an approach, in theory, should maximize benefits for developers, retailers and consumers by preventing over-provision and by providing facilities accessible to all sections of the community. In practice, problems arise over the control of demands for new shopping space from both developers and consumers whilst the developers of existing centres and the retailers within them wish usually to retain the current level of provision.

Planning shopping centres in New Towns usually involves using a series of floorspace standards related to the size of population and type of centre. The provision of shopping centres in Canberra can be used as a typical example of the policies involved and the problems encountered. Effectively from 1958 the National Capital Development Commission (NCDC) was the retail planning agency and it developed a policy involving three types of shopping district. First was the Civic Centre or City Centre which was to comprise a group of shopping centre developments with each new centre to be included in an overall city centre scheme. Secondly, there were to be regional centres (termed town centres) of around 50 000 m² and thirdly, there were small strip centres (termed neighbourhood centres) of 800 m²–1000 m². The overall plan as stated in the NCDC policy was to provide a 'limited facility in the neighbourhoods to satisfy daily needs but to restrict the provision of shops to avoid the possibility of vacant retail space with its attendant possibility of secondary low quality use'. Floorspace per head was placed at 1.11 m² comprising 0.65 m² comparison goods, 0.37 m² convenience goods, 0.092 m² personal services. The locations of the centres were determined by the master plan with the smallest centres being central to residential neighbourhoods of 4000–5000 people and within 0.8 km of households in the neighbourhood. A consultant's report in 1961, however, resulted in a change of policy. The strip centres were reduced in size to 600 m²–700 m² and true neighbourhood centres (termed group centres or intermediate centres) were introduced thus giving a four-tier hierarchy of centres. The new type of centre was designed to provide a focus for three to five residential neighbourhoods, was located accordingly and was to comprise 3000 m²–5500 m² of floorspace anchored by a 1500 m² supermarket. Although the consultant suggested a reduction in the floorspace provision per head on the assumption of increased efficiency in the retail trades, this particular recommendation was not adopted by the NCDC. Through the period of rapid expansion of the city in the 1960s this four-tier hierarchy was established.

In 1971 two planning consultants' reports were received by the NCDC and a further change of retail planning policy resulted. Future strip centres were to be again reduced in size to 350 m²–400 m², corner shops were to be built and the overall floorspace provision was to be reduced from 1.11 m² per head to 0.85 m² per head. This new figure was to be distributed through the four types of centre as:

	%	m² per head
Strip (neighbourhood) centres	20	0.17
Neighbourhood (group) centres	20	0.17
Regional (town) centres	45	0.38
City (civic) centre	15	0.13

The location principles for these centres were defined as:

1 Retail facilities within 0.8 km of all residents.
2 Group centres 1.9 km from higher order centres.
3 Group centres 2.8 to 3.2 km from town centres.
4 Group centres located at the entry/exit point of residential areas where traffic tends to gravitate, with the aim of maximizing access to centres and between centres. This is intended also to promote competition.
5 Town centres located close to the geographical centre of their potential trade areas.

Although these policies were adopted they were not always applied in development during the 1970s, particularly in the growing residential areas in the south of the city. Here a five-tier hierarchy of centres is being built with strip centres further reduced to around 250 m^2 and sometimes ceasing to be a centre but having instead a single shop. Secondly, strip centres (termed intermediate centres) of about 1000 m^2 or even up to 2500 m^2 have been reintroduced. Thirdly, group centres have been enlarged to 3500 m^2–6500 m^2 with town centres and civic centres providing the top two tiers. The effect of this change has been to increase, not decrease, floorspace per head to 1.412 m^2 as a long-term planning figure. In the short term, during the 1970s, the full development of two regional (town) centres in advance of the complete residential development of their potential trade area, the extension of some existing centres and also the unforeseen and insufficiently controlled expansion of retailing on industrial land resulted in floorspace per head rising to 1.6 m^2. This is twice that designated in the official policy and not unexpectedly several shopping centres, particularly the smaller ones, had high levels of shop vacancies. This shows the difficulty inherent in attempts to control intra-urban shopping centre location. At the time of writing a full review of retail planning policy in Canberra is underway with a first report presenting the current position already published (Capital Development Commission, 1981). It seems likely that policy change will occur. If it does, there will have been four policies within twenty years for an activity which needs several years to plan, build and establish a shopping centre. The location of centres advocated by each policy, is, however, typical of most New Town schemes in their attempt to provide centres close to residential development but distanced from each other. There is clearly a balance to be achieved between the number of types of centre, their size and their distance apart. Creating this balance is not easy when the demands of retailers for different types of space and the behaviour of consumers have been changing as rapidly as they have in Australia and Europe in the last twenty years.

Canberra's difficulties in creating acceptable plans can be seen being repeated in British, Swedish, Israeli and in American New Towns. The period between successive innovations in shopping centres, and in changes in retailing and consumer demand, is less than the time required to develop shopping centres. The problem associated with incorporation of hypermarket centres into British New Towns is an example of the difficulty of adapting retail planning policy formulated for traditional types of shopping centre to meet the needs of the newer centre types. Similarly, there have been problems involving the multi-use centres included in plans for New Town development around Scandinavian cities. These have proved to have larger trade areas and to serve more people than was anticipated at the planning stage.

The conflicts are rather fewer in societies with less intense pressures for retail change. Thus in Eastern Europe intra-urban centre location is directly related to residential development and there is not such a range of possible centre types. In Hungary the shopping centre floorspace standard in new residential areas is 1225 m² per thousand dwellings which is approximately 0.36 m² per person. This is then divided approximately on a 3:1:1 ratio betwen food and convenience goods:comparison goods:service uses. In a typical suburban development of 12 000–15 000 people in high-rise blocks a shopping centre of around 4000 m² would be provided, supplemented by a few very small units of about 10 m² each on the ground floor of some residential blocks. Within 4000 m² there would probably be two large units, a restaurant and a supermarket of less than 1000 m², with 8 or so smaller units. Such a centre is the Lublin Centre in Debrecen. The city centre shopping district provides a second tier in the hierarchy of retail provision.

Within the developed capitalist economies the conflicts between speed of innovation, length of development process and intra-urban land use planning policies have been one of several reasons accounting for the trend toward smaller centres. They are quicker to develop, more responsive to innovation and can be located within an intra-urban system of centres without major disruption to existing centres. Large centres of 100 000 m², whether multi-use downtown renewal centres or peri-urban free-standing centres, may take ten years to develop, perpetuate outmoded marketing ideas, and have a serious and disruptive impact on the attempts of land use planners to generate a 'fair and efficient' system of shopping centres in the city. This chapter has reviewed some patterns of centre location together with their causes. At the inter-regional level the major location factors are the differentials in overall regional economic development and differences in direct development costs. Government policy acts also as either a deterrent or an encouragement to centre building. At the inter-urban level additional factors are city size and the presence of local entrepreneurs willing to take risks with investment. At the intra-urban level local land use planning activities temper the processes associated with market area economics to create the pattern of centres within the city.

CHAPTER 5
THE SYSTEM OF TRADITIONAL SUBURBAN CENTRES

The series of neighbourhood, community, regional and super-regional general purpose suburban shopping centres accounts for the vast majority of centres in North America and Australia. Despite the growth in interest in the newer centre types these traditional types dominate provision in most cities with low density suburbs. There is not only the legacy of centres built over the last half century but new centres along traditional lines are constantly being added to the stock. Few, if any, cities in North America, even in the north-eastern areas of population decline, have yet achieved total market saturation in respect of traditional suburban shopping centres. In some cities development opportunities for new regional centres may be non-existent but even here scope remains for smaller centres. In Ohio, in 1981, with markets close to saturation for large centres and high interest rates, centre development has almost ceased in Cleveland and Toledo but there is still activity in smaller centres in Columbus and Akron and small centres are being built in many of the small towns in the state. There also exists the possibility of renovation or redevelopment of large centres which may now be thirty years old and losing their competitive edge. The De Bartolo Company has several remodelling schemes and some expansions of established centres underway. Other large developers are also specializing in this, witness the thirty-store expansion of the Westland Mall in Columbus and the adding of an extra 20 000 m² to the 100 000 m² Eastwood Mall in Niles. Development activity has continued with traditional centres although at a slower pace than in the mid-1970s. A system of traditional suburban centres has been developed mainly in the last 40 years in most North American and Australian cities. The aim of this chapter is to consider this system of traditional suburban centres by focusing on its competitive processes and in particular on three aspects: the creation of the system and land use zoning influences on it, the operation of centres in the system and the methods of competition adopted by centres in the system.

CREATION AND MAINTENANCE OF A CENTRE SYSTEM

Earlier chapters have reviewed the location, growth and types of centres in American cities. Within the system of traditional centres the four types – neighbourhood, community, regional, super-regional – exist and operate usually in broad equilibrium with each other. Centre development is carried out by many different companies within a city, each company seeking to optimise the financial returns on its centres. Developers, therefore, are as much concerned about the location and trading conditions in their competitors' centres as they are about conditions in their own centres. The total mix of centres within a city must operate in general equilibrium if each centre is to return a profit. There are examples of centres which have been total failures but these are relatively rare amongst the 15 000 or so centres developed in the last thirty years. Some, however, have not produced the financial return originally anticipated, whereas others have over-performed. Within a city the many individual decisions about whether and how to go ahead made by different developers together result in a broadly balanced system of centres which has, as shown in Chapter 4, certain characteristic locational patterns.

The system of centres does not depend wholly on developer decisions to keep it in equilibrium. Land use planning policies, traditionally weak in the USA, stop major disruption to the whole system. The underlying process of suburbanization and decentralization, which fuels the centre development process, is extremely persistent and is one which, arguably, has been the single most important process affecting North American and Australian cities over the last thirty years (Muller, 1981). Land use planning policies have sought to manage this decentralization process but its governing forces are outside the usual ambit of control of land use planners.

Kivell and Shaw (1980) usefully summarize the studies of retail suburbanization and consider the reasons for the process under five headings. First is the decentralization of population and consumer demand. Suburban population growth in North America is a well documented and continuing process. Vance (1976) points out that in the American city:

> The last two decades have been a time of new commercial congregation to go along with the great transformation of residential geography that came with the nearly universal use of cars, the development of a national housing policy of encouraging private ownership of single family houses, and the creation of mass production methods of house construction to keep down the cost of the product. Class specific housing tracts were the outcome of mass production . . . The mass appeal selling that formerly concentrated in the central business district has been able to move to the suburbs and there to find a threshold of support sufficient to allow the development of an integrated shopping center . . . As housing expands, the potential for new outlying shopping centers is itself expanded . . . (p. 38).

Not only has there been an absolute increase in suburban populations but increasingly they have become spatially segregated in terms of income and consequently spatially segmented in terms of consumption patterns and consumer behaviour.

The second reason is the increase in personal mobility and its effect on consumer behaviour. The construction of urban motorways has altered the actual and perceived accessibility maps of many American cities. Key suburban intersections have enhanced accessibility resulting from the design features in the motorway plans. Improved personal mobility also has been detrimental to highly concentrated retailing, usually in the CBD, both because of the demand for car park space at the place of concentration and because of the weakening of public transport networks which focus on the main activity centres.

The third reason is the unsuitability of city centres as locations for the new types of retailing which have emerged in the last twenty years. The lack of space for expansion in centres means that stores have been unable to benefit from scale economies in operation nor can they adapt to the new technologies of building and selling which have resulted elsewhere in more efficient retailing and higher returns on invested capital. Furthermore the loss of inner-city populations has removed buying power from the central city trade area. For many years, therefore, the central city steadily became less attractive as a site for shopping centre investment. Only in recent years as new types of centre have been developed has the central city improved in its commercial appeal. For the traditional general purpose free-standing centre, CBD locations are still not attractive in American cities.

A fourth reason is simply the availability of development land. This feature has been discussed in Chapter 3 and in the review of the development process (p. 39). Recent studies of the ownership of urban fringe land suggest that ownership changes occur and speculation begins up to twenty years before development takes place. By the time the developers become active, sites exist and may well have been consolidated by land speculators in earlier years. The ease of development on greenfield sites compared with the difficulties of redevelopment enhances the other factors at work creating the decentralized centre system.

A fifth reason usually put forward for the increased decentralization of retailing is the effect of institutional factors. Whilst this is a rather nebulous concept, in many American cases it means the working of the local land use zoning legislation. It is worthwhile considering this in some detail because although the other four reasons for decentralization are also present in British cities, a system of general purpose free-standing suburban centres has not evolved. Land use control mechanisms are quite different in the two countries and this difference may be considered as one of only two critical factors in retail suburbanization. While several preconditions, listed above, must exist for retail suburbanization through general purpose centre development, it will not occur without the triggers of, first, permissive land use planning machinery and, secondly, a business community strongly committed to the investment and risks involved in suburban centre development. Whilst in North American cities both triggers are present, this is not the case in Britain.

SHOPPING CENTRE ZONING

The original intent behind zoning legislation was:

> to create a logical, orderly system of land use regulation where the intended use of every property was known in advance and development would occur as a matter of right. But what has happened in the course of time is that municipalities have added to their zoning ordinances a wide variety of provisions which give more flexibility to the developer and more discretion to municipal government. In practice, municipalities have zoned undeveloped land, not for residential or commercial or whatever their ultimate purpose is to be, but rather for agricultural or some other category which serves as a holding zone (Seelig, Goldberg and Harwood, 1980, p. 90).

This approach has the advantage of allowing planning agencies to wait and see and make a final decision when permission for development is requested. The rigidity of the old zoning method when the future use of each plot was clearly stated has been softened by the new approach, but at the cost of introducing delays into the planning system as developers specifically have to seek development permission through an application for re-zoning, or zoning variance or other special permit. The second advantage of the current approach to zoning policy is that it allows greater opportunity for mixed use development on large sites. Heeter (1969) usefully reviewed the problems of the zoning system and the ways it can be improved. With a more sophisticated and complicated development process, some change in the rigid procedures was necessary and inevitable.

Several approaches have been adopted to providing more flexible zoning. Three in particular are of interest for shopping centre development. Whilst particularly appropriate to newer centre types they also allow a more flexible approach to the zoning of traditional type centres. First, *floating zones*, which are:

> areas with a set of purposes defined in the zoning ordinance but without specific boundaries delineated on the zoning map. When there is an opportunity to carry out the intent of the floating zone on a particular tract of land, the council or other legislative body amends the zoning ordinance to specify the boundaries of the zone. For example, the legislative body may create a floating zone for a large shopping centre development. It considers such a district desirable but wishes to wait until a proposal is made for a particular location (Seelig, Goldberg and Harwood, 1980, p. 93).

Such a zoning procedure is particularly applicable to rapidly expanding cities where many development opportunities exist and where the acceptability of a development may depend on what other schemes are underway. The land use planning agency can apply more sensitive policies by having floating zones in which specific projects are granted permission on merit rather than automatically being deemed to meet zoning requirements as in traditional zoning practice.

A second more flexible zoning technique is the use of *planned unit development*. By allowing the designation of an area for planned unit development the zoning agency effectively allows a mixed use development on the zoned tract. Planned unit developments are large comprehensively-planned developments which include a variety of residential types, each of which might be zoned separately in the traditional approach, and also of commercial uses. The design and location of the different uses within the overall tract is the responsibility of the developer rather than the zoning agency but in almost all cases the developer works closely with planners in the zoning agency to produce an acceptable mixed use scheme. There are clear opportunities for shopping centre developments in areas zoned for planned unit development. There can be either a local centre to provide for residents within the residential sections of the scheme or a larger centre to provide also for other nearby residential areas. In North Dallas, for example, where rapid suburban expansion took place in the late 1970s, several tracts have been zoned for planned unit development and shopping centres have been built as integral parts of mixed density residential suburbs.

The third form of flexible zoning is more applicable to speciality centre development than to general purpose free-standing centres but is worthy of a brief mention. This is the idea of *transferable development rights* which allows the right to develop land to be severed from a piece of land and transferred to a nearby, usually adjoining, piece of land. The mechanism is used in some American cities by creating conservation zones and transfer zones. The development rights from conservation zones are moved across to transfer zones so allowing higher density development in the transfer zone and lower density in the conservation zone. In the case of the preservation of a historic structure for use as a speciality shopping centre, for example, the development rights of the historic building site may be transferred to an adjacent site thus reducing the pressure for redevelopment of the historic site. All three forms of flexible zoning attempt to allow development to break out of the straightjacket of fixed zoning where uses are attached to specific and often small pieces of land.

Within any of these zoning schemes it is unusual for land to be zoned for a shopping centre. Instead it is zoned for commercial use: 'only coincidentally does a sufficiently large size for a major centre exist within an existing commercial strip or highway commercial zone . . . A shopping center zone can be introduced into commercial zoning as a special use district (which then becomes a floating zone) for which a re-zoning application must be filed with the approval authority' (McKeever, 1973, p. 22). For community and regional centres, and even for the larger neighbourhood centres, rezoning applications almost invariably are required before development can proceed. McKeever's comprehensive review of land use zoning from the shopping centre viewpoint suggested that the following seven features of a re-zoning application were the important ones considered by planning commissions.

1. *Substantiation of the need for a centre.* This will be based on market analysis and the degree of tenant interest. It is not the purpose of the land use commission, however, to protect the developer from making commercial mistakes. The extent to which zoning may serve to control competition has been the subject of considerable legal debate in the USA. Two types of case are usually distinguished: first, problems associated with the *proximity* of the proposed development, where objections are made because the trade area of the proposed centre would overlap with that of an existing centre such that neither would compete successfully; second, problems associated with *demand*, in which an assessment of the community provision of centres suggests that there is no scope for a further centre. Control of competition of the first type has been ruled unconstitutional by courts in many states but the second type of problem is one with which zoning deals. Given the success in many cities of centres located adjacent to each other then doubts must be cast on the legitimacy of the proximity problem. The second type of problem involves general questions of land use welfare and the limitation of economic dislocation in a community. Studies by Mandelker (1962) and Tarlock (1970) illustrate these issues; the latter study was concerned with the phasing of decisions to allow new centres to be developed in an expanding community. Control of competition may be a factor in zoning but it may not be the dominant purpose of zoning.
2. *Site area suitable to the type and building area of the centre.* It is usually considered important that the site is in one piece and not crossed by major highways.
3. *Location and access to the site is not hazardous.* As the proposed centre is likely to be a major traffic generator so traffic flow considerations are important in re-zoning applications.
4. *On-site parking is adequate.* This condition is usually met through the application of defined standards.
   Factors 2, 3 and 4 are concerned with the particular site under consideration and how it is to be developed as a parcel of land.
5. *Land use within the plan comprises suitable functions and arrangements are adequate for interior site circulation.* Not only is the tenant composition of the centre scrutinized by the re-zoning committee but so also is the design of the circulation system, both pedestrian and vehicular. Arrangements for servicing the stores and for emergency service access are considered.
6. *The building group has architectural unity and is aesthetically satisfactory.* There is control over details of design to halt, at an early stage, any architecturally substandard layouts.
7. *Impact of the development on adjacent uses.* This is particularly important with nearby residential areas which may be affected adversely by noise, car fumes, sign displays etc.

Factors 5, 6 and 7 are concerned mainly with the design and function of the building complex rather than with the site itself.

The re-zoning application covering the seven points is reviewed in public and a recommendation made to the legislative body on the re-zoning proposal. If successful the site is re-zoned and the development process can move forward along the lines described in Chapter 3, with the land use planner being involved at various stages over detailed conditions which might be integral to a granted permission. These may well be spelt out in ordinances and involve the adherence to various standards including landscaping, sign provision, etc. The re-zoning procedures are a common feature in centre development because of the frequently large scale of the projects and the small plot size, and because of the limited land use types defined on most zoning maps and general zoning policies. Whilst traditional zoning procedures are rather restrictive and rigid in their application, the flexibility provided by the re-zoning mechanism and by the newer types of zoning methods allow much greater negotiation between developer and planner. Flexibility produces a more sophisticated, wider-ranging system of general purpose free-standing suburban centres which is probably better from the consumer's viewpoint.

FEDERAL ENVIRONMENTAL PROTECTION POLICIES

'At one time, zoning was virtually the only approval required before submission of plans for a building permit' (Urban Land Institute, 1977, p. 53). Not only is there now more federal legislation with which to comply but 'the same forces that have created sophisticated consumers have created concerned citizen groups who are ecologically aware and aesthetically responsible' (p. 53). In some cases consumer groups have been able to set up planning boards with executive powers in zoning affairs. More important, however, is federal legislation and in particular a group of laws passed in the early 1970s dealing with the environmental impact of large projects (notably the Clean Air Act of 1970 and amendments of 1977). Later the Community Conservation Guidance legislation was in operation from November 1979 to June 1981, and had an important effect on centre projects during its period of effectiveness.

The Clean Air Act requires state agencies to review, before construction, indirect pollution sources which include shopping centres, because of the pollutant emissions of cars using the centre. The Act provides considerable power to the states to allow them to influence the siting of such pollution sources as large free-standing shopping centres. The Community Conservation Guidance policy did not specifically mention shopping centres but resulted in twenty-four economic impact statements on proposed centres being prepared in less than two years. The policy aimed to:

1. Prevent federal actions from affecting adversely existing urban centres.
2. Prevent federal aid program from being counter-productive by working against each other.
3. Provide a rapid review machinery for major new commercial developments.

A central review agency was set up to consider proposed major developments, frequently shopping centres, in which federal assistance was required. This assistance was often in the forms of funding highway improvements or granting a permit for environmental works or other site improvements. A proposed scheme was referred to the review body only when requested by the chief elected official of any community which might be affected by the proposal. The review agency then prepared an analysis of the likely economic impact of the proposal and so of the consequences of the federal involvement in the scheme. In the light of this analysis changes in the proposal could be required before development permission was granted. As originally conceived the policy was considered as a way of protecting city centres from large centres in the suburbs but the final form of the policy was much weaker than the original drafts. The existence of the policy was more important than its implementation in that it increased develper awareness of the likely impacts of new schemes. The repeal of the policy on the recommendation of President Reagan's Task Force on Regulatory Relief was welcomed by centre developers. During its two years the policy had not only delayed some suburban developments but had also encouraged developers and planners to see suburban centre developments as part of a metropolitan system of centres complementing, as well as competing, with each other.

The land use control system, in its various guises, has not served to limit suburban shopping centre development in North American cities to any marked extent. Individual locations have been subject to state and city controls but the overall shift in emphasis from city centre to suburbs has not been subjected to control except for the ill-fated federally-based Community Conservation Guidance policy. The land use control procedures have been permissive to the processes creating a demand for centres in the suburbs and developers have responded to this demand.

OPERATION OF THE CENTRE SYSTEM

To allow assessment by both developers and planners of the likely effect of a new centre being added in the suburbs several analytical techniques have been developed. The one most widely used was formalized by Huff (1962) and later adapted by Lakshmanan and Hansen (1965). There have been numerous attempts to improve this model but the simpler forms still are these most widely used. In the Huff version of the model, which he used primarily to designate the intra-urban trade areas of shopping centres, the expected number of consumers, E_{ij}, resident in a zone i and likely to travel to shopping centre j is considered proportional to the number of consumers in zone i (C_i) and to the probability (P_{ij}) that a consumer at i will select centre j. Therefore:

$$E_{ij} = P_{ij} \cdot C_i$$

The probability P_{ij} is considered to be the ratio of the utility of centre j compared with the other (n) centres which Huff calculated as:

$$\frac{S_j}{T_{ij}^{\lambda}} \bigg/ \sum_{j=1}^{n} \frac{S_j}{T_{ij}}$$

where S_j is the size of centre j
T_{ij} is the travel time for a consumer to move from zone i to centre j
λ is a parameter, to be empirically estimated, which reflects the effect of travel time on various kinds of shopping trips.

Huff tested the model for a number of individual centres but it is possible to extend the model to describe an equilibrium pattern in a system of n centres and m zones by introducing the constraint that:

$$\sum_{i=1}^{m} C_i = \sum_{j=1}^{n} E_j$$

or that the number of people visiting the centres is the same as the total number of people resident in the zones. More recently retail expenditure has been substituted for the number of people and the model is assumed to describe the distribution of consumer expenditure amongst competing shopping centres. The model is simple, perhaps too simple, in considering centre sales as a direct function of centre size and the population distribution around the centre. Various criticisms of the approach have been summarized by Kivell and Shaw (1980) who suggest that such models will not provide a framework for the analysis of centre location despite their use as aids to decision making by planners and developers alike. Although the model does not describe reality, if it is used by decision makers then it does nevertheless affect whether or not centres are developed at particular sites. In some cases the use of the model has served to underpin planning decisions although, as pointed out in Chapter 4, the principles of centre location are more complex than those described in this model.

The institutional permission, via the zoning process, for the growth of general purpose free-standing suburban centres is one feature of the development of this centre type in the USA. Secondly, the operation of the centres has to be such as to yield a continuing return on capital investment. The regular reports produced by the Urban Land Institute in the *Dollars and Cents of Shopping Centers* show the operating costs and the revenue from general purpose, neighbourhood, community and regional shopping centres. Within a competitive system of centres, which are in effect investments, operating costs have to be controlled and individual centres operated at a profit. As can be seen in Table 5.1 there is considerable difference in receipts, expenses and operating balances amongst the three centre types. Although in the smaller centres dollar amounts per square metre generally are lower, the proportionately lower land and building costs within total capital costs generate operating per-

Table 5.1 Operating results in relation to capital cost for regional, community and neighbourhood shopping centres (median values): 1966–81

CENTRE TYPE	1966		1972		1981	
	$ per m² G.L.A.	%	$ per m² G.L.A.	%	$ per m² G.L.A.	%
Regional centres						
Total Capital Cost	186.2	100	NA	100	NA	100
Operating receipts	21.4	11.5	26.0	15.6	75.8	18.1
Operating expenses	7.1	3.8	9.1	5.1	29.4	7.4
Operating balance	14.3	7.7	16.1	10.4	43.2	10.0
Community centres						
Total capital cost	152.8	100	NA	100	NA	100
Operating receipts	19.9	13.0	22.0	15.6	37.5	18.3
Operating expenses	6.6	4.3	7.4	5.1	10.9	5.1
Operating balance	13.3	8.7	14.4	10.8	25.8	12.3
Neighbourhood centres						
Total capital cost	150.7	100	NA	100	NA	100
Operating receipts	20.9	13.9	23.3	15.1	43.8	18.6
Operating expenses	6.8	4.5	7.4	4.1	11.3	4.6
Operating balance	14.0	9.4	16.1	9.8	32.2	13.8

NA = not available
Source: Urban Land Institute (1966), (1972), (1981)

centages comparable with larger centres. Generally the operating balance as a percentage of capital cost has increased over the last twenty years. The operating balance is not the actual return to the shopping centre owner. From this operating balance depreciation, finance costs and tax payments have to be deducted in order to calculate a net return. Neighbourhood centres still compare favourably with regional centres when this is carried out. From the 1972 data, for example, after deductions from the \$16.1 per m² operating balance in both regional and neighbourhood centres, the net operating income was \$3.88 per m² for the regional centres and

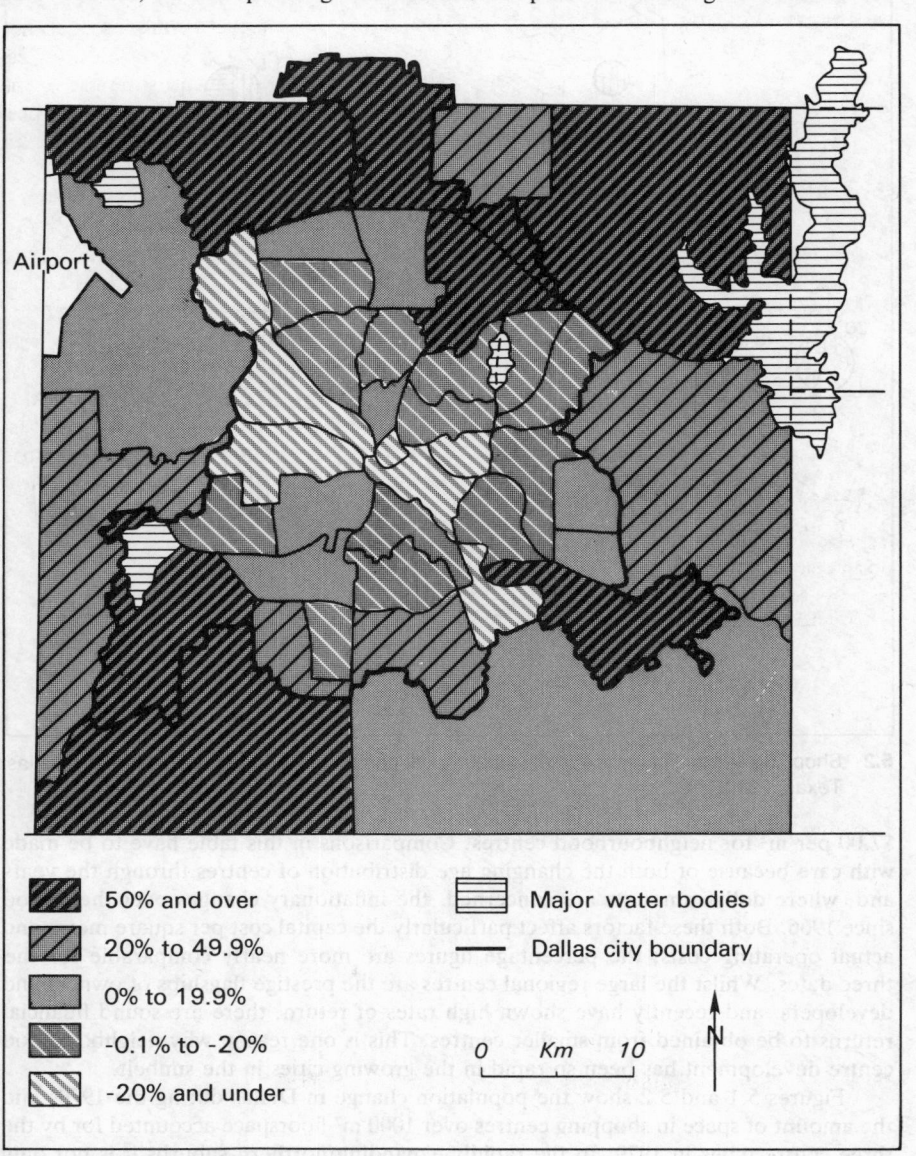

5.1 Population change in Dallas, Texas.

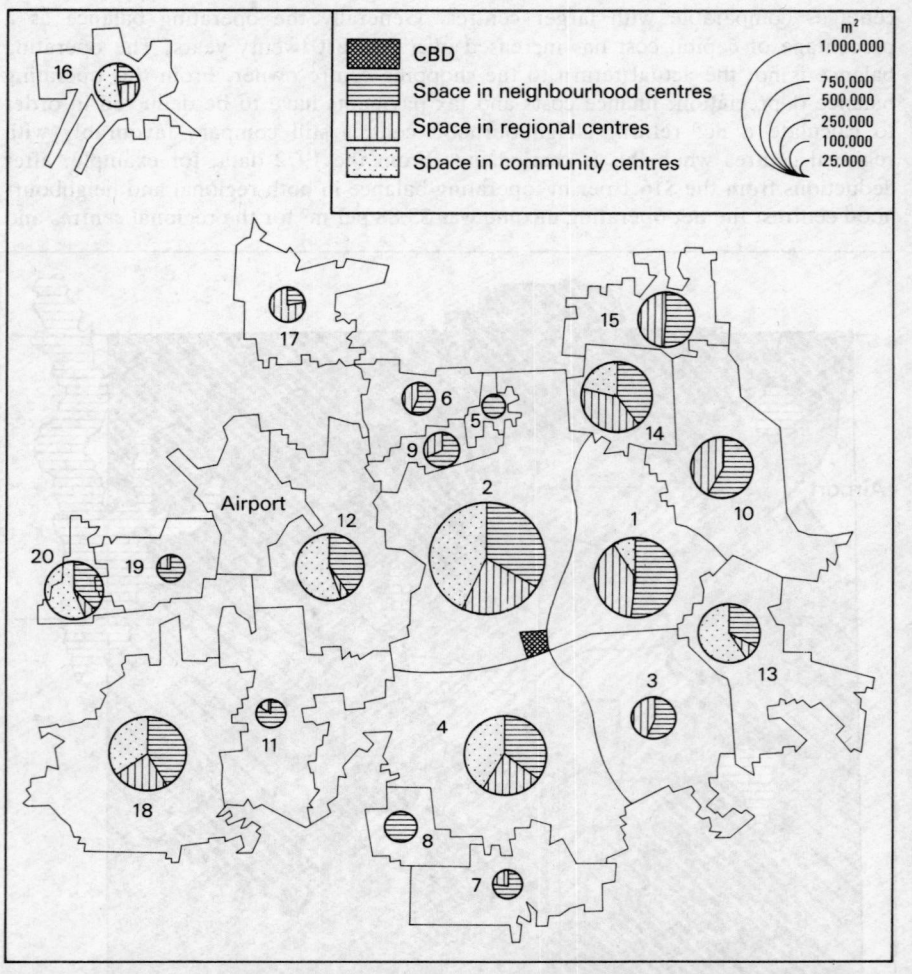

5.2 Shopping centre floorspace in neighbourhood, community and regional centres in Dallas, Texas, 1980.

$7.00 per m² for neighbourhood centres. Comparisons in this table have to be made with care because of both the changing age distribution of centres through the years and, where dollar amounts are concerned, the inflationary changes over the period since 1966. Both these factors affect particularly the capital cost per square metre and actual operating costs; the percentage figures are more nearly comparable for the three dates. Whilst the large regional centres are the prestige flagships of owners and developers, and recently have shown high rates of return, there are sound financial returns to be obtained from smaller centres. This is one reason why neighbourhood centre development has been so rapid in the growing cities in the sunbelt.

Figures 5.1 and 5.2 show the population change in Dallas during the 1970s and the amount of space in shopping centres over 1000 m² floorspace accounted for by the three centre types in 1979. In the rapidly-expanding northern suburbs it is not only regional centres, such as Prestonwood (see Fig. 3.4), which have been developed but

Table 5.2 Change in floorspace in shopping centres over 1000m² in Dallas, Texas, built during 1979

ZONE	NEW SPACE OPENED (m²)	CHANGE IN VACANT SPACE (m²)	NET ABSORPTION	ABSORPTION %	% OF TOTAL FLOORSPACE VACANT
1	42 651	18 899	23 752	26.8	15.4
2	191 355	11 220	180 135	82.0	3.8
3	7 525	−2 983	10 508	69.0	4.1
4	6 675	868	5 807	18.4	5.8
5	13 656	204	13 451	82.9	10.2
6	12 723	−31	12 754	79.1	6.5
7	1 022	−3 918	4 940	53.6	10.1
8	5 665	−944	6 608	70.7	4.4
9	0	2 924	2 924	79.9	1.1
10	17 144	−173	17 318	53.7	6.4
11	0	−1 268	−1 268	0	5.5
12	3 493	9 264	−5 771	0	7.8
13	0	−8 628	8 628	48.8	3.8
14	42 825	13 096	29 729	48.5	9.8
15	63 447	10 369	53 077	67.8	13.6
16	89 193	6 716	83 477	91.4	5.7
17	1 858	−959	2 817	35.6	6.8
18	30 377	5 914	24 463	52.1	5.3
19	2 035	68	1 968	38.7	8.2
20	5 920	186	5 734	57.4	2.2
TOTAL	537 565	57 513	480 051	60.8	6.5

Notes: Zone numbers refer to Figure 5.2
Source: based on data obtained from Henry S. Miller Company, Dallas

also a plethora of neighbourhood centres have been built both on commercially zoned land at suburban road intersections and also as integral to planned unit developments. In the lower-income areas of the city and the districts of population decrease it is the regional centres which are missing from the centre system not the neighbourhood centres. The data on which Figure 5.2 is based does not include small strip centres of less than 1000 m² GLA. Table 5.2 shows the amount of new space in centres over 1000 m² built during 1979 and the absorption of this space. The figure includes extensions as well as new centres and absorption is a measure of the extent to which new space has been fully incorporated into the centre system. Absorption is calculated simply as increased space minus increased vacancy of alternatively increased space plus decreased vacancy. In the whole of Dallas, for example, during 1979 shopping centre space increased by 537 565 m² and the amount of vacant space increased by 57 513 m² so net absorption was 480 051 m². This can also be calculated as a percentage of total vacant space giving a percentage absorption of 60.8 per cent for Dallas. The zone numbers in Table 5.2 refer to the zones shown on Figure 5.2. As might be expected, absorption rates are related to patterns of population change. Retailers move to fill centres in areas of growing population but move out of centres in zones of decreasing population. The release, during 1979, of an enormous amount of space in north Dallas is shown in the figures for zone 2. Absorption of this new space into the centre system was high and reflected retailer perceptions of market potential in this area of rapid growth of middle-class housing. Absorption was rather lower in the north-east zones of Plano (15) and Richardson (14) with here some development being carried out in anticipation of rapid population increase in 1980, 1981 and 1982. In the Denton zone (16), beyond the continuous built-up area, new space was almost completely absorbed into the system with the opening of the community's first regional shopping centre in 1979.

THE RENOVATION OF CENTRES

The vacancy and absorption rates not only reflect the changes occurring in the system of centres in terms of market potential but also reflect the quality of retail space provided in the centre. Because the quality of space declines with the age of centre and retailer demand for facilities in the centre also changes, so the renovation and renewal of centres must take place for them to continue to be profitable trading environments for retailers. Within systems of general purpose suburban centres in the USA there are now considerable pressures for the renovation of the older centres of all types. Not only do the centres not satisfy the needs of present day retailing but the tenant mix may no longer be the right one to serve the surrounding suburban area which may well have changed its demographic composition since the centre was built. Centres developed in areas of young families in the early 1960s have by the 1980s a trade area comprising people at the 'empty nest' stage of the life cycle.

The periodic up-grading of a centre to improve its physical condition and to enhance its competitiveness can provide the opportunity for a complete re-leasing of the development and a significant increase in operating income (Koltz, 1973; Lion, 1976). The Panorama Mall, north of Los Angeles, provides an example of the 'growing number of economically stable but badly aging properties that are being revitalized across the country' (Warner, 1981, p. 79). It dates from 1955 and by the late 1970s was deteriorating, physically and economically. The 28 000 m² centre was sold for $6 million in 1979 to a joint venture group consisting of a developer, who specializes in used centres, and a finance group. The new owner has renovated the centre, enclosed it and added a further 5200 m² of space at a cost of $7 million. The renovation has involved a fundamental redesign of centre space from one 20 000 m² department store and 13 other store units to the department store, 51 other units and 8 small kiosks each of 10 m². Centre enclosure has enabled evening trade to grow because shoppers are generally unwilling to use open centres after dark, whilst the broadened base of the tenant mix provides scope for promoting the centre as a unified shopping area. The financial feasibility plan for the centre suggests that average sales per square metre will double as a consequence of the renovations to an estimated $2200 per m². The emergence of developers specializing in renovation projects proves they can be financially viable. Before taking on a scheme the renovator of centres such as Panorama Mall:

> makes an in-depth analysis of what the property is worth, how much money needs to be invested to substantially improve return on investment and exactly what will be done with the center once acquired. If all the factors aren't properly weighted and the numbers carefully calculated, a developer could end up losing money or defeat the purpose of enclosing and upgrading such a mall (Warner, 1981, p. 81).

Similar conclusions are reported in other studies of centre renovation such as the financial feasibility study in Applebaum and Kaylin (1974) and the studies of South Shore Mall, Long Island and Green Bay Plaza, Wisconsin by Chase (1979). There are generally five benefits a developer can obtain from a renovation scheme, assuming the correct centre for renovation is chosen:

1. The existing location may be very advantageous with the centre having been developed at a time of less competition for sites. Such a prime location would not be available for new development.
2. The existing centre has an established identity which can be used as a basis for the promotion of the renovated centre. Unlike new centres, in a renovation it is not necessary to establish a new identity for the centre.
3. There are likely to be fewer zoning and environmental agency problems with a renovation than with a new centre development.
4. Lower average construction and finance costs are likely for renovations than for new centres.
5. Considerable scope is provided for a new tenant plan which may benefit from the provision of more small specialist units in the centre and for increasing retail income. An older 30 000 m² centre may have average rents about $30 per m² whilst in a new centre the rate may be $50 m² and the higher rate may be more appropriate for the renovated centre.

Heirich (1979), a developer specializing in renovation schemes, has provided an analysis of common mistakes in such schemes and how to avoid them and suggests that they should be evaluated in a logical and progressive way comparable to, but not the same as in, new centre development. He suggests that 'to upgrade an older center will normally yield a much better return on investment than the same dollars invested in a new center project' (p. 138). With the high nominal interest rates in the American economy since the late 1970s there has been a natural unwillingness to seek finance for major projects but renovation schemes, where the solid return on a smaller investment can begin within a year, are proving popular. The presence of older centres in need of upgrading, the economic viability of renovation and the state of the loan market have combined to create a surge of redevelopment activity amongst all sizes of general purpose free-standing centres in suburban America.

COMPETITION FOR CONSUMERS

Redevelopment is aimed at enhancing the competitive position of a centre within the system of centres in a city. There are many forms that this competition can take but certainly with larger centres it is competition amongst the centres, rather than competition at store level, which is the dominant competitive process. It is not unusual for branches of the same chainstore to operate in competing centres. Inter-centre competition is limited, therefore, in respect of price but is instead based on the tenant mix, location and the non-retail services and activities available to users of the centre. Amongst the smaller centres, retailer image is probably more important than centre image and in these cases price competition is intense, for example, supermarket chains anchoring neighbourhood centres.

Competition amongst larger centres aims both at increasing the degree of penetration in the established trade area and at extending the trade area. The positive attributes of a centre's location, particularly its accessibility, are stressed in attempts to extend the trade area whilst the quality of the shopping experience is stressed in attempts to increase market share from within the trade area (Lewison and Showalter, 1977). In this second case it is therefore the personal and social motives for shopping rather than the utilitarian ones on which competitive activities are based.

Surveys of shopping behaviour in general, many of them based on interviews in large suburban centres, have suggested at least six personal and four social motives for shopping and these motives are reflected to different degrees in inter-centre competitive activities. These personal and social motives complement the purely economic one of having to make a purchase. The operation and the design of regional centres reflect the competitive activities. The six personal motives for shopping identified from surveys are:

1. Obtaining personal knowledge of new trends and fashions. Visits are made to 'see what is new'.
2. Self-gratification. A bored person may seek stimulus in shopping or someone depressed purchase personal items to raise morale. Visits are made to 'make you feel better'.
3. Diversion from the routine of daily life. Informal or free entertainment may be provided and visits are made 'for a change'.
4. Role playing. Visits to a centre may be an integral part of having a particular position in society with the visit being 'expected of me' as a housewife or a teenager.
5. Activity. Visits may be made for the benefits obtained from 'having a walk' around the centre.
6. Stimulation of the senses. The constant sensory bombardment which occurs on shopping visits may result in some visits being made 'just for the kicks'.

Visits to shopping centres are made for a combination of these personal motives and also from the more social motives of:

7. Making social contacts. Visits to a centre may provide the opportunity for a variety of social contacts with friends, acquaintances and new contacts.

8. Social contacts with peer groups. A shopping centre, or a store in the centre, may provide a meeting place for a peer group.
9. Social status. Visits to centres may be the result of a desire for status both by mixing with people of different status and perhaps gaining perceived status by having shops and the centre woo the shopper.
10. Participation in a social event. Visits to centres may result simply from a wish to be involved in society and participate in bargaining and trading activities.

Although these various motives may exist for any shopping trip, the designers and operators of shopping centres, particularly of the larger ones, have to respond to them in order to increase the numbers of visitors. The enclosure and the interior design of centres together with the control of the atmosphere in the centre create a shopping environment in which sensory and social stimuli can be carefully managed. Large malls may be carpeted to make the activity attraction stronger, promotions are mounted to enhance the diversionary attraction, music may be played to stimulate the senses, meeting places and message boards can be provided for social contacts to be made and for peer group messages to be relayed, centre advertising may stress status considerations, whilst general design features try to create an environment which will make visitors 'feel better' for their visit.

The system of general purpose shopping centres has transformed retail provision in American suburbia in the last forty years. The centres have become totally integrated into both the suburban economy and society by providing nodes of employment and investment and by acting as a focus for social interaction. The emergence of a system consisting of several centres of each of the three types around major cities has naturally generated competitive processes amongst centres. Centres compete for visitors who, it is hoped, will be shoppers. Location is a major factor in this competition and zoning practices have a strong influence on location and hence competition. Competition is apparent in the operating results of centres, their vacancy rates and in their development in the expanding sections of suburbia. The design and operation of centres, particularly of large centres, also show the awareness developers have of the competition for shoppers amongst centres.

The suburban centres have became the suburban community. They are no longer part of the community, they are the community. Rouse (1963), one of the early developers of large centres argued that, 'The success or failure of a regional shopping center won't really be measured by the character of its architecture or the balance sheet of the center; it will be measured by what it does for the people it seeks to serve' (p. 100). The caricature of the regional centre as a great cash register in verdant suburbia may now be replaced by the image of the centre as a space station with a full life-support system acting as a refuge for travellers through urban space. American suburban society has become dependent on these social stations both large and small. In the larger ones the environment has been carefully created with strict control over the various stimuli present. The regional shopping centre has become a social laboratory in which participants react in controlled ways to given stimuli. Whether the cremation of such artificial environment is good or bad, whether there should be ground rules on their management, whether they should be rejected or encouraged, become moral questions which society must answer. In the meantime, however, the system of general purpose free-standing centres continues to underpin the lifestyle of American suburbia.

CHAPTER 6
FOCUSED AND RENEWAL CENTRES

Shopping centres of most types have been developed in all countries with an established shopping centre industry. The general purpose suburban centre is most intensively developed in the USA but other countries may be considered the type areas for other forms of centre. Focused centres and central area renewal centres are most widespread in Europe. This chapter considers these two centre types in their type areas.

FOCUSED CENTRES

Focused shopping centres have a single dominant mass-merchandising anchor tenant complemented by a small number of retail and service traders. It was pointed out in Chapter 2 that there are a number of possible types of anchor tenant for these centres and tenant mix in the smaller units is carefully controlled to complement the merchandising mix and policy of the anchor. The anchor tenant, almost invariably, is aiming at a mass market and is using *scrambled merchandising* methods. A food-based anchor unit, for example, will also be marketing a carefully controlled range of convenience non-food products including clothing, hardware, toys, etc., whilst a hardware-based anchor will probably also retail a range of convenience food products. This movement away from the traditional lines of goods to a mixed range typifies scrambled merchandising. The widespread acceptance of scrambled merchandising within the retail trades has been one factor in the development of focused shopping centres. It also underpins one of the major problems posed to land use planners by the building of these centres. In adopting mass merchandising and scrambled merchandising policies the retailers require large shop units and the space for these units can often only be found in suburban centres. The retailers are heavily influenced by the general factors of retail suburbanization outlined in the previous chapter, and because of the focus on mass appeal convenience goods, the large units can have a major effect on trade patterns of other retailers selling convenience goods with consequential disruption of established commercial land use relationships. The most common form of focused centre is that based on a hypermarket and the impact of hypermarkets on urban land uses in general has become an issue of considerable concern to land use planners.

Focused shopping centres have become increasingly common since the mid-1970s in all countries with an established shopping centre industry. In the USA their development can be seen as a method of centre diversification in areas of traditional centre saturation and also the focused centre is proving to be a way of tapping the market potential both of the lower-income areas of cities and also of the middle markets. The policy of having a wide product range but comparatively narrow brand mix, which typifies anchor tenants in these centres, appears economically viable to retailers in lower-income and smaller trade areas yet also appears to be a method of providing essential, low-price shopping facilities to previously disadvantaged consumers. Typical of this centre type in America are a series of centres developed by the Rouse Company in association with existing Clover discount stores. A small enclosed mall of around 5000 m² is added to the large free-standing discount store providing an opportunity both for discount store renovation and for an additional thirty or so small units to complement the discount operation. The Rouse Company appear to have considered this innovation in response to the lack of sites left for regional centres in the north-eastern states. Early consumer surveys suggest that shoppers to large regionals may well use such focused centres for convenience goods since the weekly patronage patterns of the two centre types complement each other. Within Australia also the development of these centres in middle markets has been extensive but has highlighted the land use planning problem – a number of centres have had serious consequences on the vitality of the central shopping district of small towns. In Britain the planning issues have been more firmly faced and relatively few large centres have been allowed to develop. Land use planners have succeeded in limiting the size and sales mix of the anchor tenant, so reducing impact elsewhere in the retail system, and also they have incorporated social provision into the focused centres so providing what have been termed as *district centres* (Antill, 1981; Unit for Retail Planning Information, 1977). These consist of a focused shopping centre, usually based on a small hyper-market, located in association with centralized service functions such as schools, a community centre and medical and cultural facilities. The strict control allowed within the land use planning legislation in Britain (see p. 98) has allowed planned provision of focused centres in limited numbers.

Development in France

It is in France however that focused centres evolved most rapidly in association with the expansion of hypermarkets since the late 1960s. It is worthwhile therefore to concentrate attention on France's development and control processes. Since the late 1970s a few focused centres in France have opened with anchor stores other than hyper-markets, but by a mid-1981 there were estimated to be 230 focused centres in France, over 200 of which were anchored by hypermarkets. A hypermarket is usually defined as a retail unit of at least 2500 m² sales space, selling a wide and low-price range of food and a general range of non-food products. Self-service trading methods are used throughout the store with payment for goods through an integrated series of checkouts which frequently are part of sophisticated point-of-sale data collection and analysis system. A scrambled merchandising policy based on price competition is the basic sales policy of hypermarkets. Car parking associated with the store is provided and is generally at least three times the sales area of the store. Hypermarkets, therefore, constitute a retail form which attracts large numbers of car-borne consumers and is designed to handle high volume sales. As an anchor for a focused centre such a store is ideal and it soon became apparent in France that hypermarkets could be integrated into the shopping centre concept.

The Carrefour company was the innovator of the hypermarket. The company began when a food wholesaler and a non-food retailer joined forces and began a company to operate supermarkets. The first Carrefour supermarket opened in 1960 and although relatively small (650 m²) it differed from existing French supermarkets in being built on the outskirts of the town (Annecy), in having a relatively-large car park (eighty cars) and in operating a discount price policy. The supermarket made a rapid impact on the traditional retail provision of Annecy which led the operators to consider merchandising non-food goods on the same principles. In the 1960s non-food discount stores were growing in number in the outskirts of many North American towns and a significant advocate of this type of retailing was the National Cash Register Company and especially Trujillo. Carrefour directors were influenced strongly by this one man and, after a visit to North America, they opened in June 1963 their first discount store, a copy of the American type of operation, at Sainte Geneviève de Bois. It was a 2500 m² store and had parking space for 450 cars, but, unlike other stores of that size was on the edge of a town of only 12 500 people. The break with traditional retail practice was total and it was almost five years before Carrefour had any competition in France from other operators. It was during this period that the concept of the hypermarket emerged as it moved away from a simple copy of the American discount store to become a retail style in its own right.

Entry into hypermarket operation was rapid, however, once it got underway in the late 1960s and by 1973 over 200 units were trading. Not all were focused shopping centres, though, and the early stores were free-standing units. Experiments in some of these early units introduced kiosks and very small concessionary stores into the hypermarket, creating shops within the store. A second step was the creation of a small number of shops, six or eight, outside the hypermarket but part of the same building complex. The focused centre idea was developed and the centre design was amplified so as to include the small units within a fully integrated, often enclosed centre with a controlled operating environment. Figure 6.1 shows a typical end result of this evolutionary process. In this example the hypermarket is the dominant element in the centre, with associated smaller units and on the same site there are the related garden centre, petrol filling station/tyre bay, etc. Developers of these centres, in most cases, were the operators of the hypermarket which, in the specific case of Figure 6.1, was a consumer-cooperative organization. The dynamic for centre development has come, therefore, from the retail organizations who, encouraged by their success, have developed the concept of the focused centre. Fewer than ten major groups are

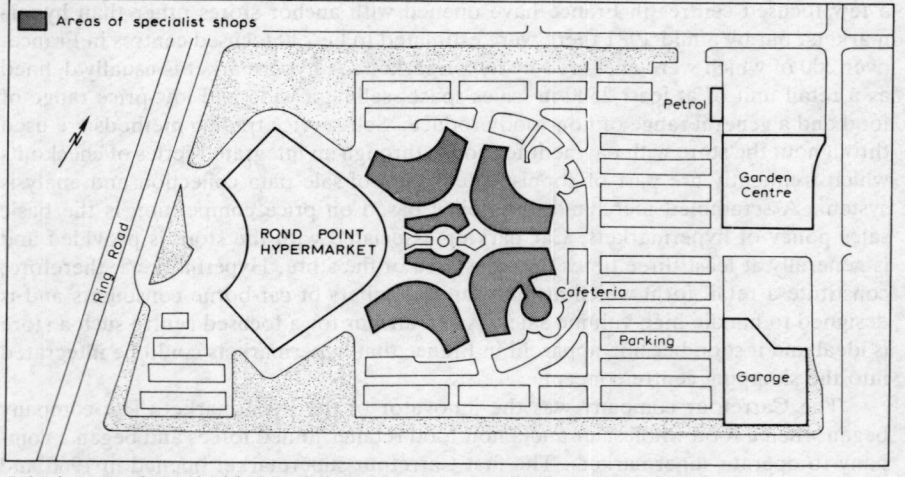

6.1   Layout of a typical focused shopping centre based on a hypermarket.

involved including the consumer-cooperative movement but they account for over 70 per cent of the hypermarket-focused centres operating in France in 1981. It is now unusual for major operators such as Carrefour, Euromarché, Cora, Auchan, Rallye, or companies associated with Paridoc, to develop hypermarkets outside a shopping centre format. In recent years these companies have begun renovating early-built free-standing hypermarkets to create a focused centre. The Rallye at Brest, for example, which opened in 1968 with 7000 m² sales space and a very small group of associated units was renovated in 1980 not only to increase the hypermarket sales space to over 8000 m² but also to increase the number of complementary units and increase their combined floorspace to over 5000 m². It is interesting to surmise whether with reno-vations and extensions on this scale the resulting shopping centre may still be con-sidered a focused centre or whether it has effectively been transformed into an American-style community centre. With 5000 m² of non-hypermarket sales space ten-ant mix begins to change and branches of national retail chains become interested in locations in such centres. The tenant mix no longer simply complements the hyper-market but becomes itself capable of attracting consumers to the centre.

A study carried out in 1978 of investment costs in various types of retailing in France (*Libre Service Actualité*, 1978) analysed the development costs of free-standing hypermarkets and hypermarkets in focused shopping centres. Some key findings of that study of twelve hypermarkets of each type are shown in Table 6.1. As with the financial studies reported for North American centres, however, the investment cost figures must be considered critically because the sample of French centres includes examples developed between 1969 and 1976. In general, the figures of focused centre investment relate to more recent developments and as such are affected by inflation, as all costs are in current figures. Nonetheless, the figures provide a guide to the scale of investment in these developments. Within the focused centres communal areas were greater and more space was given over to car parking but hypermarket size tended to be lower than with free-standing stores. Land and buildings costs, related to sales space and total development costs for focused centres, was notably more

Table 6.1 Investment costs of hypermarkets in free-standing and focused centre locations 1978

	FREE-STANDING	WITHIN FOCUSED CENTRE
Sales floorspace of hypermarkets in sample (m²)	8485	7285
Sales space as % building area	59	55
Sales space per parking place (m²)	7.0	8.3
Total land costs per m² (francs)	112	79
Construction costs per m² of building (francs)	854	1109
Costs per m² floorspace (francs)		
Land acquisition	710	778
Site works	750	876
Construction	1437	2008
Fitments	1428	2010
TOTAL	4325	5672
Capital cost depreciation as % sales value	1.30	1.89

Source: Libre Service Actualité (1978)

than for free-standing units, although the income generated by the extra units offsets the increased costs. The study showed that if the income from the additional units is not considered then investment costs are covered by gross margin receipts in 358 days in free-standing units but in 499 days in focused centres. The conclusion is, therefore, that hypermarket investment in free-standing units is to be preferred from a purely financial viewpoint but the analysis ignores the additional income accruing to the developer (usually the hypermarket developer) of the focused centre from the rents of the associated retail and service units. A critical aspect of the management of these centres therefore is the calculation of tenant mix and tenant selecion policy. With the appreciation of the importance to total operating receipts of the rent income from associated traders so there has been a tendency to increase the number of these associated units in the centre and to move away from the original idea of a focused centre totally dominated by a single store.

Tight control of tenant mix aroused objections from the independent retailer lobby. There was considerable debate on tenant selection policies as it became appreciated that hypermarket operators and centre developers in choosing tenants for focused centres naturally were favouring chain store operations with their higher rent paying capacity, greater customer appeal and more effective retail management methods (Libre Service Actualité, 1981; Liepmann, 1973). Not only was the hypermarket in the centre having an adverse impact on independent traders in established shopping districts in the trade area of the centre but also the opportunity to relocate to within the centre was not available because these locations were let to non-independent traders. The advantages of location in focused centres is shown by the very low rates of tenant change. In the twenty-one centres associated with Auchan hypermarkets there are almost 600 smaller units and, according to data from Auchan, tenant change is only 3.5 per cent per year. Although it is claimed that independent traders are well-represented in these centres in effect the majority of units are let to branches of chain stores. Usually, however, the question of tanant mix is not simply one of a choice between chain and independent retailer but is one of assessing the retail potential of individual operators. A well-managed progressive independent trader would, in most cases, be given the same consideration as a branch of a retail chain but by the very nature of the retail industry such independents tend to develop into chains and so tenant mix, as discussed in Chapter 3, appears bereft of independent operators. The strength of the small shopkeeper lobby in France, however, was sufficient to achieve, in 1973, control legislation of hypermarket-based centres.

Developers' and hypermarket operators' awareness of the importance of the associated retailers encouraged them to increase the space given over to these smaller units. Table 6.2 shows the number of hypermarket centres developed in two time

Table 6.2 Size of hypermarket-based centres in France 1966–73

DATE OF CENTRE FORMATION	CENTRE SIZES					
	Less than 10 units		11–25 units		26–40 units	
	No. of centres	No. of shop units	No. of centres	No. of shop units	No. of centres	No. of shop units
1966–70	9	80	21	375	6	194
1971–73	12	83	23	419	19	630

periods before the advent of controls. The average size of centre increased from 18 to 21 shops over the two time periods and the increased share of larger centres is clearly noticeable. The size of the anchor tenant was also increasing during this period so that the larger centres tended also to have larger hypermarkets, some having over 10 000 m² sales area. Additionally the growth in actual numbers of smaller centres was particularly rapid in the early 1970s as the centres spread through the French urban system and began to be developed in middle markets. Figure 6.2 shows for two periods the spread of the small centres through France. Between 1966 and 1970 there were only four centres in towns of less than 50 000 people but in the second period a further twelve such towns acquired centres. Although there was continued expansion in the Paris, Nord–Pas de Calais and Marseille regions the general pattern was one of rapid decentralization into middle markets and even into small towns.

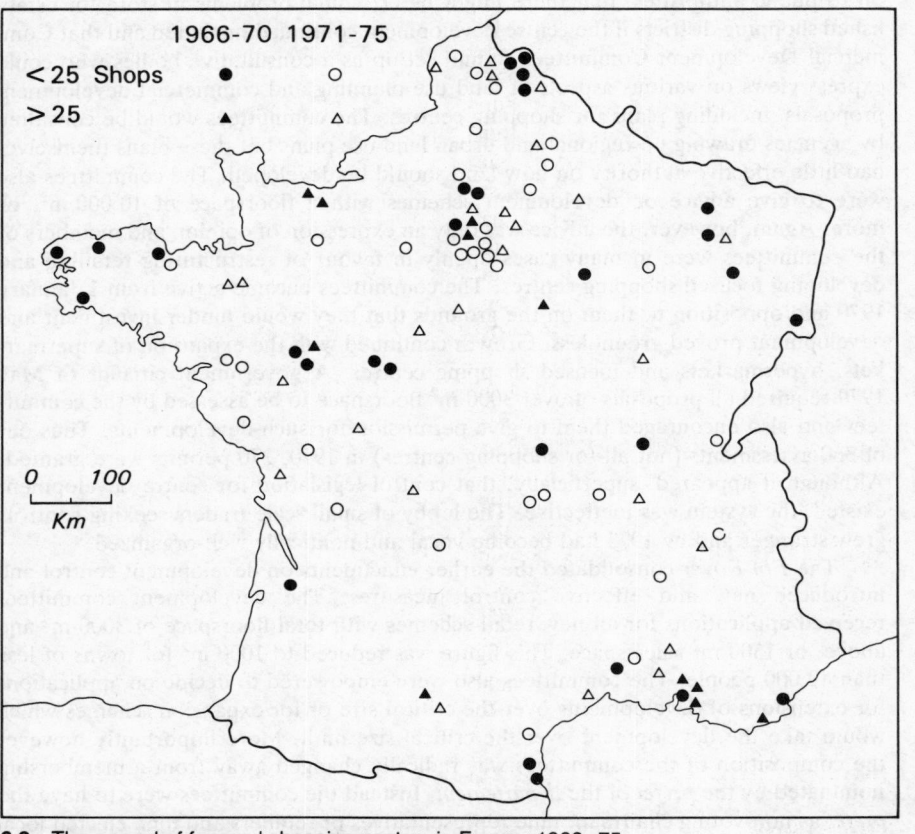

6.2   The spread of focused shopping centres in France, 1966–75

French controls on development

The rapid growth in numbers of hypermarket centres, their impact on established shopping districts, the outcry over tenant selection policy, the increasing size and spatial spread of centres and the realization that such centres were forming the nuclei of small towns, 'in a sense, mini-towns based on hypermarkets – but without homes'

(Qualité, 1974, p. 58), all combined to result in governmental intervention and the control of the development process. The *Loi Royer*, named after its originator, is a complex piece of legislation aimed at intervening in a number of aspects of retailing in France. Beaujeu-Garnier and Bouveret-Gauer (1979) have described the social, economic and commercial planning articles within the overall act. In respect of focused shopping centre development the Loi Royer, in articles 28 to 36, strengthened and gave real powers to the Commercial Development Commissions which had been set up earlier in each of the 95 French *départements*. During the late 1960s there was growing awareness within the government that the distributive trades were undergoing radical structural change. In 1969 a government circular on 'The role of commercial infrastructure in town development' suggested that some social costs associated with new centre developments should be carried by private enterprise and not be passed on to public authorities, that there might be economic problems in store for established shopping districts if the centre development continued unabated and that Commercial Development Committees should set up as a consultative bodies who could express views on various aspects of land use planning and commercial development proposals, including plans for shopping centres. The committees would be consulted by agencies drawing up regional and urban land use plans but these plans themselves had little effective authority on how land should be developed. The committees also were to give advice on development schemes with a floorspace of 10 000 m², or more. Again, however, the advice was only an expression of opinion and members of the committees were in many cases openly in favour of restructuring retailing and developing focused shopping centres. The committees became active from 1 January 1970 and opposition to them on the grounds that they would hinder investment and development proved groundless. Growth continued with the expansion of supermarkets, hypermarkets and focused shopping centres. A government circular of May 1970 required all proposals of over 3000 m² floorspace to be assessed by the committees and also encouraged them to give permission for such developments. Thus out of 360 assessments (not all for shopping centres) in 1970, 270 permits were granted. Although it appeared, superficially, that control legislation for centre development existed, the system was ineffective. The lobby of small scale traders seeking controls grew stronger and by 1973 had become vocal and politically well-organized.

The *Loi Royer* consolidated the earlier enactments on development control and introduced new and effective control measures. The development committees received applications for all new retail schemes with total floorspace of 3000 m² and above, or 1500 m² sales space. This figure was reduced to 1000 m² for towns of less than 40 000 people. The committees also were empowered to decide on applications for extensions of developments over the critical size or for expansion schemes which would take the development over the critical size limit. More importantly however the composition of the committees was radically changed away from a membership nominated by the *préfet* of the *département*. Instead the committees were to have the *préfet* as non-voting chairman, nine representatives of retailers and nine elected local representatives, including the mayor of the commune where the proposed scheme was located. A subsequent amendment enlarged the membership by the addition of two representatives sponsored by consumer organizations. It is not unusual for elected local representatives to be independent retailers and so the small shopkeeper lobby was strengthened considerably with the new committees. All proposals for focused centre developments and for extensions and renovations since 1973 have been dealt with by these development committees who consider applications in terms of three broad criteria:

1. national levels and trends of retail and commercial activity;

2. the evolution and structure of retailing in the *département*;
3. the balance amongst the types of trade in the *département*.

Having considered an application the committee can accept or reject the application, but in the case of rejection there is a right of appeal. The appeal may be initiated by the potential developer or any group on the committee and appeal is made to the appropriate central government minister; the final decision is made by a ministerally-appointed committee with a similar balance of membership to the development committees.

The effect of the *Loi Royer* was an immediate reduction in the rate of development of focused shopping centres. The speed of development has slowed, but it is debatable whether there are now fewer focused centres in France than there would have been without the law. Some market analysts suggest, probably incorrectly, that in 1981 market saturation was close for this type of shopping centre and that, without the control mechanism, saturation would have occurred a few years earlier than it will now do. It seems more likely that growth will continue for some years yet. Freis, (1978) who was responsible for the central administration of the policy, commented in 1978 that the law 'did no doubt have the effect of slowing down the building of hypermarkets, but nevertheless about 100 hypermarkets have been built since it came into force. It is not therefore a question of systematic blockage, rather that of an additional obstacle which businesses have to overcome.' He further argues, that 'The rate of new building would have slowed down in any case, even without the Loi Royer, since sites suitable for new building are increasingly rare, competition is more and more lively, construction costs are higher and a certain stagnation in consumption due to the economic crisis leads promoters to be cautious' (p. 45). There remains nevertheless considerable pressure for new development. There were over 120 applications for hypermarkets considered by the committees in 1980. All but a few of these involved focused shopping centres. Measured in terms of floorspace only 23 per cent was given permission but this still represents, when the centres are complete, an average rate of opening of more than one new focused centre every fortnight. Even with the new developments which have been allowed market saturation for focused centres based on hypermarkets is still some way off and developers are keen to obtain permission before saturation is approached. There is thus a danger that a control mechanism such as the *Loi Royer*, which responds to applications for permission rather than indicating locations for development, encourages competing developers to request more development than they really need on the assumption that they will obtain permission on perhaps only a quarter of their applications. Under such circumstances it is difficult to gauge what density of hypermarket-based centres the market will bear and over-provision can occur despite the control measures.

Studies of the general effect of the *Loi Royer* polity have suggested five themes apparent in its operation (Dawson, 1982; Hermand, 1975). The five trends are applicable to varying extents to focused shopping centres. First, through the 1970s there was a steady decline in the number of applications for development. There was a sharp increase in 1980, sustained in the early part of 1981, after this consistent decrease. A number of the major French retailers and store developers were reviewing their operations in the late 1970s, consolidating their market positions and preparing development plans. The Europe-wide slowdown in economic growth also probably accounts in part for the slowing in development activity. Secondly, there has been a steady increase in the refusal rate for development permissions. With focused centres this refusal rate rose from around 60 per cent in 1975 to almost 90 per cent in 1979. If hypermarket permissions in total are considered the range is not as great but there is still a noticeable increase. The reduction in available acceptable sites is probably the cause of this trend. Thirdly, there is considerable difference in acceptance rates for different types of application. Hypermarket-based centres have the highest refusal rates. Other focused centres appear to have lower refusal rates and permissions for extensions are relatively easy to obtain. Fourthly, it appears to be easier to obtain permission for the smaller developments than for large ones. Committees are required to take into account, in coming to a decision, the likely impact of the proposal on existing patterns of provision. They take decisions to minimize disruption to the existing system of stores and centres and so they favour the smaller schemes. Fifthly, an increasing number of decisions are resulting in ministerial appeals. Through the 1970s there was a real chance of a developer overturning a refused permission by seeking an appeal. A much tougher line has been taken since 1980 with far fewer ministerial rulings changing committee decisions. Whether this will result in a reduction in the number of cases taken to appeal awaits to be seen. The overall results of the *Loi Royer* policy since 1973 have certainly been to slow the rate of development of focused shopping centres, to create smaller new centres and to encourage renovation and extension of existing centres.

The election of a socialist government in France in mid-1981 caused some confusion over the implementation of the *Loi Royer* policy. Almost immediately on taking office, the new government suspended until further notice all development permissions for new focused shopping centres. Each committee was also required to prepare an inventory of centres and other large developments in each *département* and also to prepare a plan to guide future retail development. These plans will then provide the basis for future decisions on development applications. It seems likely that under the new government the development committees will be required to take a more positive role in the planning and control of focused centre development in France. The committees were being required to produce these plans quickly so that a national coordinated policy of retail development in general could be formulated during 1982 and within this plan focused centres are likely to be important. Also it seems likely that the concept will evolve further along a path towards the greater integration of social service provision into the centres. In this respect there are likely to be parallels between future centres in France and the newer centres of this type in Britain.

CENTRAL AREA SHOPPING CENTRES

In the classification presented in Chapter 2 three sub-types of central area shopping centre were identified: infill, extension and core replacement centres. In Europe these developments have become an integral and accepted part not only of urban land use planning policy but also of urban lifestyles. From the planners' viewpoint the goals of central area schemes are the resolution of land use conflicts in the urban area and the achievement of some socially *optimal* distribution of retail facilities. From the viewpoint of the city government, to whom the planners are responsible, the goals are both the promotion of the town's commercial activity and the enhancement of the image and prestige of the town within the framework of a European urban culture. This consciousness of an essentially European urbanism is important for it was instrumental in the decisions to re-create city centres and provide a centralized structure for cities after the Second World War rather than to follow the North American trend toward a decentralized city structure of suburban activity centres and a decentralized pattern of urban government. Gosling and Maitland (1976), writing of the post-war birth of central area schemes in Britain, considered that 'The wholesale disappearance of city-centre shopping facilities during the war, to be followed by their wholesale replacement, produced new agencies of large-scale development whose activities continued beyond the reconstruction period to provide the framework for almost all postwar integrated centre developments' (p. 87). Such a view point is applicable to the other European countries which suffered major war damage to their city centres. With the initial stimulus taking place in city centres a self-perpetuating process was initiated which resulted in continued renewal of town centres based on the goals of urban planners and elected urban governments.

City centre renewal and shopping centre provision marked as 'progressive' the towns which had positive land use plans and a concern for the living conditions and lifestyle of the residents. Resolution of land use conflicts was seen by many planners in terms of encouraging a centralized city with a dominant city centre. Transport plans were formulated to these ends and the optimal distribution of shopping facilities included a large renewal centre within the central area. By focusing attention on the central area redevelopment, these schemes became prestige symbols of the town, symbols easily perceived by city government and voters. City government became financially involved in these centres, stimulating a policy of protecting such centres from suburban competition and effectively resolving conflicts in favour of the city centre. Given the initial activities of centre developers and land use planners in 1945, particularly in Britain but also elsewhere in Europe, the subsequent focus on central area renewal schemes was almost inevitable. The town centre schemes required the active participation of planner, developer and finance agency. Architectural input came from local government and the developer and property expertise came from the development company. The functions of those in the web of the development process shown in Figure 1.3 were present but the individual institutions took time to emerge. Writing of the late 1940s Gosling and Maitland (1976) argued that:

> The tripartite arrangements, whereby local authorities assembled large sites by the use of CPOs (compulsory purchase orders) and provided a planning framework, and the private development companies carried out the work funded by financial institutions, proved irresistible. For the new development companies it was reinforced by the system of building licenses, which were only granted for replacing bombed shops or shops for new housing estates, so that cooperation with local authorities was essential. On the strength of their early projects at Bristol, Plymouth and Exeter, Ravenseft, the first company in the field, went on to conclude agreements with local authorities in Hull, Swansea, Sheffield, Sunderland and Coventry (p. 88).

The active role and powerful position of land use planners and local government in general differentiates the European and particularly the British position from that in the USA.

In the USA it is only in relatively recent years that the power of the land use planner has increased, and central city schemes have got underway. Midtown Plaza in Rochester, New York, lays claim to be the first core replacement centre in the USA and this centre opened in 1962. By 1970 there were a dozen developments which could be classified as core renewal or central area extension centres. Almost half these were in the state of Connecticut, where land use planning legislation has been introduced to limit the spread of free-standing general purpose suburban centres. During the 1970s considerably more schemes were developed elsewhere as city government responded to federal initiatives to improve central city environments after the 1968 inner city riots. The land use planner, therefore, has been able to take a more active role in the centre development process and encourage location in central areas. This change in position of the American planner is shown in a review of the central area renewal centre concept by Alexander (1975). Many planners and developers are suggesting that during the 1980s central area renewal schemes of all types will become much more common in the USA. If such is to be the case then there are lessons to be passed on which have been learnt in over twenty years of development of these centres in Britain. Within Britain, since the formalization and consolidation of land use planning legislation in 1947, urban planners have been the dominant institution in the centre development process.

The planning framework for central area renewal centres in Britain

A thorough and excellent review of British central area renewal schemes is provided by Bennison and Davies (1980). The planning framework for centre development is essentially the same as for any other form of land development. Within the application of this general legislation via land use policy, Bennison and Davies suggest a change in emphasis in centre planning since about 1965. They argue that:

> First, there has been the evolution of town centre plans with their emphasis on redevelopment and a segregation of land uses; second there has been a series of *ad hoc* policy directives, largely issued through Development Control Policy Notes from central government, indicating how local authorities should react to new retailing pressures in suburban areas. To a large extent, the two sets of influences have followed consecutively on each other, the former dominating retail planning policies in the first half of the post-war years, the latter those policies applied since 1965 (p. 11).

The power to control and guide shopping centre development in Britain lies with local government planning agencies through their implementation of the various Town and Country Planning Acts and their responses to central government policy circulars. Before 1947 land use planning legislation was not consolidated and was linked to a variety of public health and housing acts. The 1947 Town and Country Planning Act repealed all previous land use planning legislation and, in summary, had two main effects. First, it required anyone wishing to develop land, in any way including changes of use, to seek permission for the development. Development was defined as 'the carrying out of building, engineering, mining or other operations in, on, or under land, or the making of any material change in the use of any buildings or other land'. Secondly, it required local government authorities, through their planning departments, to carry out a survey of their area and to prepare a development plan. The development plan was to consist of a map and written statement showing how it was proposed that land would be used in the future. Of more specific importance to shopping centre development the 1947 Act allowed authorities, as part of the development plan procedures, to designate Comprehensive Development Areas (CDAs) within towns and to obtain land by compulsory purchase in order to develop according to a town centre plan. Specific advice was given by central government on the use of compulsory purchase associated with the designation of CDAs to redevelop central areas. The early renewal shopping centres made extensive use of these features of the 1947 Act.

The development plan procedures in the 1947 Act were increasingly criticised during the 1960s and resulted in a new Act which redefined, radically, the idea of the development plan. The Town and Country Planning Act of 1968 with consolidated amendments in 1972 retained the basic idea that all development should require permission but introduced the idea of *structure* and *local* plans to indicate future development patterns. The need for change resulted from three factors: an increasing unwillingness to accept the considerable delays in arriving at decisions in the older system; an awareness, as the system was operated, that the planning mechanism was good for controlling undesirable development but poor for promoting desirable schemes, and, thirdly, a demand for greater public participation in planning decisions. Shopping centre developments were important in this last respect because some decisions by the planning authorities caused considerable public controversy when old, sometimes architecturally interesting, familiar town centres were replaced by new and unknown shopping centres (Amery and Cruikshank, 1975). The new scheme was to have structure plans containing the broad statement of general policy, showing past trends and indicating the basic pattern of future development together with local plans which contain the detailed discussion and implications for a specific small area of these general policies, and this allowed greater scope for public involvement. By the late 1970s a number of structure plans were complete, many were still in preparation, but in most cases it is the local plans now in active preparation, dealing with topics such as amounts of retail floorspace, types and locations of shopping centres, etc., which are going to determine the planning framework of British shopping centres in the 1980s.

Alongside the new Act and operating as a control measure during the change from the old scheme were a series of policy guidelines issued by central government. These constitute the second set of influences on central area renewal shopping centres suggested by Bennison and Davies. Development Control Policy Note 13, issued in 1972, required local government to submit for scrutiny any application it received for new retail development over 4645 m² (50 000 ft²). This size limit was changed in 1976 to 9290 m². The effects of this and other policy notes was consciously to discourage shopping centre development outside established shopping districts and so to concentrate developers' attention on central area schemes. This was apparent not only in structure plans and policy notes but also in the reports of the inspectors hearing appeals against refusals of planning permission for suburban centres. Again Bennison and Davies summarize the position:

> The effect of this collective body of professional opinion was therefore to force private developers to introduce most of the new covered shopping centres into existing central areas. A vast expansion in the number of these took place in the 1970s, with an increasing trend for bigger and more sphisticated schemes to be built towards the end of the decade. This in itself required a new collaborative spirit between the developers and local authorities, with the latter in a better position to acquire land and also able to assist in the acquisition of financial support (p. 14).

A more detailed review of the framework of retail planning is provided by Guy (1980) and by Wade (1979), both of whom highlight the consistent planning policies, over the last thirty-five years, of encouraging renewal centres in existing shopping districts and discouraging new centres outside the established hierarchy of retail districts. Wade states baldly that 'The planning machinery has become a system for reinforcing the existing hierarchy . . . and allows only those new centres which fit this pattern to be developed' (p. 59). Land use planning through a negative control function has taken a deterministic role in the location of shopping centres. It cannot, however, take this role in the total development process since other institutions, such as those controlling the finance or those generating ideas, have the power to drive or stop the overall development process.

Within the legislative framework different cities and regions have adopted rather different policies to solve the common problems of retail provision. It is these specific local land use planning policies which ultimately control shopping centre development. Within London, for example, the Greater London Development Plan (GLDP) of 1969 is effectively the structure plan for Greater London. Each of the thirty-two London Boroughs produces local detailed plans for their own area and create their plans themselves subject only to them not conflicting with the GLDP. Within the GLDP twenty-eight established shopping areas are nominated as *strategic* shopping districts. With few exceptions these districts were already, by 1969, the most important shopping areas in London outside the CBD. Each of these strategic districts would have retailing to serve at least 200 000 people and the floorspace in these centres would be expanded by extension centres and the facilities would be redesigned by the encouragement of core replacement schemes. Six of the strategic shopping areas were considered more important than the others and were designated *major strategic* shopping districts. The six are Croydon, Ealing, Ilford, Kingston, Lewisham and Wood Green and these form a ring around London in its middle suburbs. Each of the major strategic districts was expected to have facilities for 750 000 people, and again extension, infill and core replacement centres were envisaged as ways of redesigning the shopping districts (Ognjenovic, 1980). One other shopping centre location was nominated in the GLDP and this was outside any established shopping district. At this site in North London the Brent Cross shopping centre was developed as a free-standing general purpose regional centre. Approximately eighty other, non-strategic, shopping districts were defined and the underlying principle in the plan was that investment would be concentrated in the strategic and major strategic districts rather than in these smaller districts. The responsibility for drawing up plans for development in the strategic districts rests with the boroughs in which the shopping districts are located.

In the implementation of this plan for shopping the Greater London Council (GLC) has limited direct control. In many ways it acts in an advisory capacity but no effective intervention in borough plans is possible if the plan conforms to the GLDP strategy. Only with large developments in excess of 20 000 m² floorspace (23 200 m² before April 1980) are Boroughs obliged to seek the advice of the GLC. In one way, however, the GLDP has a direct influence on the creation of renewal shopping centres – through the designation of fifty-five Action Areas. Within these defined areas it was planned to begin comprehensive redevelopment schemes during the 1970s and some of these areas comprise shopping districts. For example the action area of Bromley town centre, in middle suburban south-east London, involves redevelopment of a strategic shopping district. The plan states 'It is proposed to develop a civic centre to centralize administrative services at present dispersed through the borough, to provide for additional shopping space to meet the needs of an expanding population, to relieve the High Street of through traffic, to provide car parking and to improve environmental conditions generally'. The designation of such action areas points to those locations where investment in renewal shopping centres is likely to be encouraged. Again, however, it is the boroughs which are responsible for drawing up plans for the action areas. A number of renewal shopping centres have been built in Greater London mostly since the preparation of the GLDP. Figure 6.3 shows the centres of over 4500 m² floorspace and also includes the Brent Cross Centre which is the only centre over 45 000 m² floorspace. For the size of the city there have been relatively few centres developed but plans now exist, at different stages, to develop at least twenty new centres of various sizes before the mid-1980s. The slowness of operation of the development process in London has been mentioned previously (Ch. 4); the land use planning system is, in part, responsible for this.

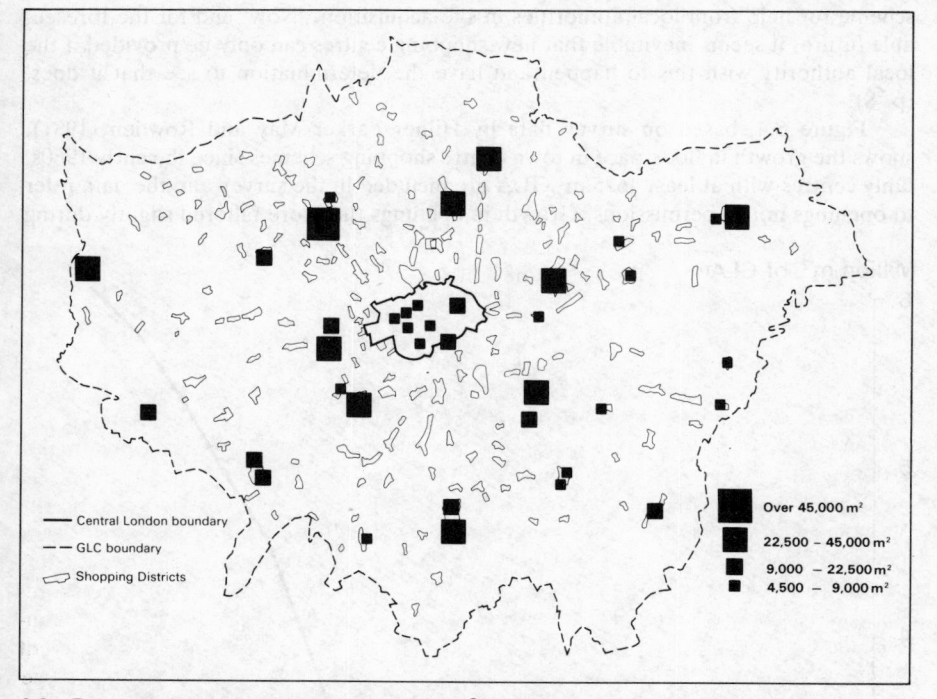

Central London boundary
GLC boundary
Shopping Districts

Over 45,000 m²
22,500 – 45,000 m²
9,000 – 22,500 m²
4,500 – 9,000 m²

6.3   Renewal shopping centres of over 4500 m² floorspace in Greater London, 1980.

The number and extent of renewal centres

After the development of the few early centres of the 1950s, the pace of centre planning quickened during the second half of the 1950s and into the 1960s. This was due not only to the increasing acceptance of the concept of renewal centres but also to four other factors. First was the abolition, in 1954, of the need for special licences for new shop building. Secondly, there was a change in the investment market with increasing amounts of finance becoming available and a switch taking place from residential to commercial property investment (see Ch. 3). Thirdly, there were retailer demands for additional retail floorspace in response to increases in consumer disposable income. Fourthly, the growth in car ownership was resulting in traffic congestion problems in traditionally-designed shopping districts and renewal, involving vehicular pedestrian segregation, was an attractive solution. Initially the plans for new centres came from local authority initiatives but the movement progressed so that initiatives increasingly came from an emerging group of centre development companies. The plans resulted in the building of over 250 centres within the decade from 1967. Since the early 1970s there has been a further swing in this pendulum with increased joint development between local authority and centre developer (Marler, 1971). Northen and Haskoll (1977), themselves developers, argued that greater joint participation in schemes was inevitable particularly for the larger and complex core replacement schemes. Writing in 1977 of the previous decade, they suggested that 'shopping centre development was invariably instigated and financed by property development companies. Increasingly, however, local authorities wished to have a greater involvement in the development than could be achieved by the exercise of their powers as a planning authority'. The developer had been willing to trade complete control over the scheme for help from local authorities in site acquisition. 'Now, and for the foresee-able future, it seems inevitable that new shopping centres can only be provided if the local authority wish this to happen and have the determination to see that it does' (p. 8).

Figure 6.4, based on survey data by Hillier Parker May and Rowden (1981), shows the growth in floorspace in town centre shopping schemes since the early 1960s. Only centres with at least 4625 m² GLA are included in the survey and the data refer to openings not to permissions. Growth in openings therefore faltered slightly during

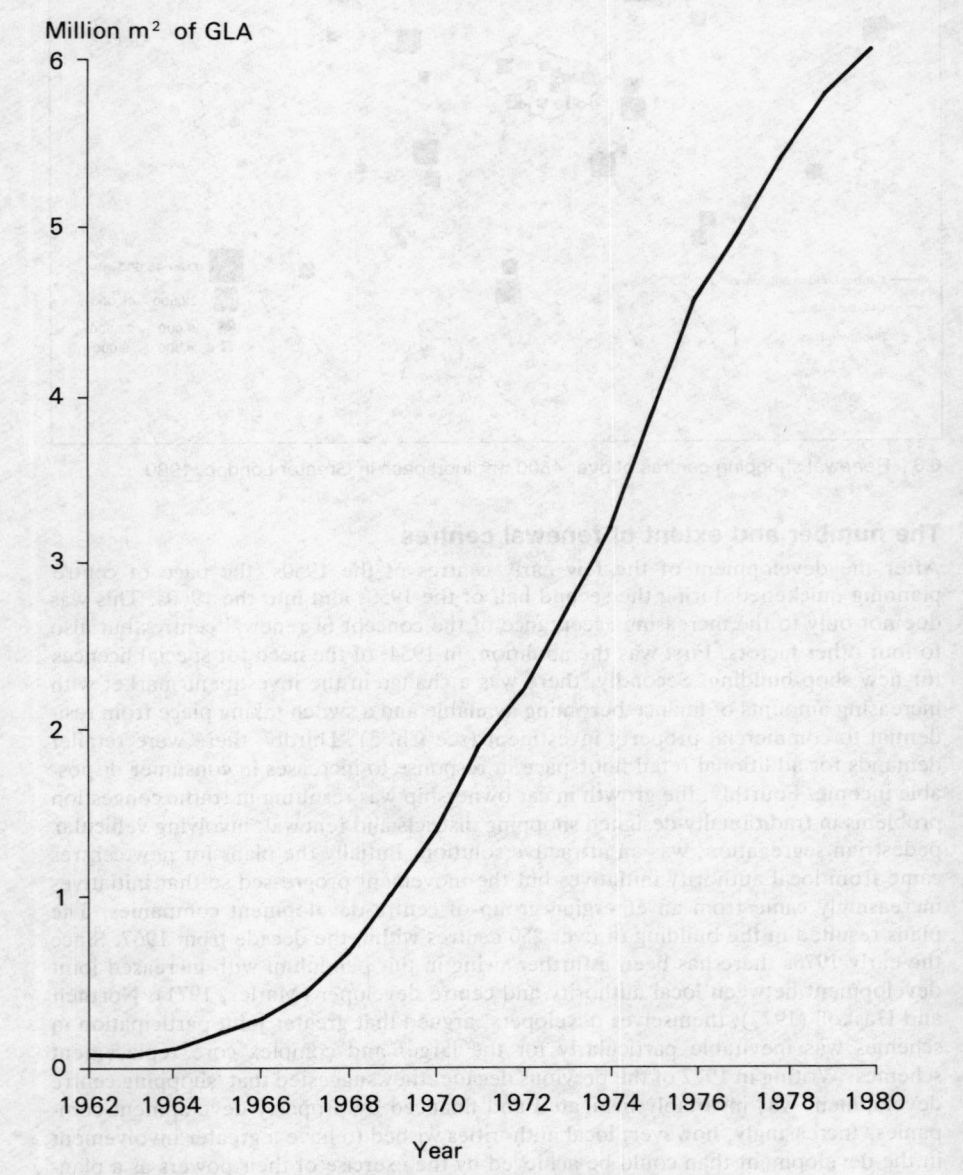

Million m² of GLA

6.4 Growth in floorspace in renewal shopping centres in Britain, 1962–80.

1977 as the effects of the economic disruption of 1973 and the property market collapse of 1974–75 passed through the system. The curve form has similarities to a logistic curve with gradual early growth followed by a period of rapid growth bounded by two clearly defined turning points. The lower one is about 1967 whilst the upper one has yet to be achieved. Undoubtedly there is a limit to renewal centre floorspace in British cities but given current permissions and plans this upper limit is some way off. Renovation and redesign of some of the early centres is already underway and whilst this is not always associated with increased floorspace there is commonly some limited expansion of a centre during renovation even if it is only a more effective commercial use of the same gross building area. Thus we may expect the increase shown in Figure 6.4 to continue for some years due both to renovation of existing centres and to development of new centres, particularly in middle markets.

As the development of renewal centres has taken place the concept has evolved of newer centres having a different form and operational character from the early schemes. Bennison and Davies (1980) and Davies and Bennison (1979) have provided an excellent review of the changing physical characteristics of renewal centres and there is little point in reproducing their study in detail. In summary they have isolated trends towards a more complex plan form for centres, an increasing proportion of enclosed centres and more non-retail uses being incorporated into the design. Amongst the changing operational characteristics, their surveys show increasing local authority involvement, greater integration with the host shopping district and increasing sophisticated tenant and lease policies operated by the developers. The increased sophistication of the shopping centre industry in Britain is apparent in many studies of renewal centre development.

Linacre (1980) suggests this sophistication results from the considerable change in general economic conditions prevailing in Britain between the early 1960s and late 1970s. Developers have responded by analysing their projects in a much more detailed fashion; analysis has become possible because of the experience developers and local authorities have gained over the last twenty-five years. Developers have come to realize, for example, that the different types of renewal centre have different critical cost factors in their development. For medium-sized infill or extension centres close to the focus of shopping activity there are usually strong design constraints imposed either by the site or by the planning authority. Furthermore tenant and retail structure may be predetermined by conditions elsewhere in the shopping district. The key factor for commercial success here is land price or ground rent for the centre site. In a larger project in a middle market or lower-income town, land price is not the critical variable nor is construction cost, which can be carefully controlled. Here the key factor is rental income coming from the right tenant mix and rent level (Centre for Advanced Land Use Studies, 1975). In major core replacement schemes, although tenant mix is important, the rents will have been subject to intensive negotiation and so the critical variable is the cost of the finance required to undertake the scheme and, related to this, the length of time that construction finance is needed. Changes in interest rates or construction delays can have major effects on the commercial viability of these large schemes. The cost escalation of the core replacement scheme in Cardiff provides an example of how the financial viability of a large centre was undermined and resulted in a quite different development ultimately being constructed (Dumbleton, 1974). It is interesting to note that in focused shopping centres, in contrast to renewal centres, the key development factor is actual construction cost. Land costs are relatively small, rental income is determined by negotiation with the anchor tenant and short-term finance is readily available. In the different types of renewal centre however different elements of overall costs become the critical cost variable.

The impact of renewal centres

Part of the reason for the overall increase in sophistication of centre developer activities is the awareness and assessment of the impact of renewal centres. Both land use planners and developers have become increasingly conscious that renewal centres, particularly large ones, have a plethora of intentional and unintentional effects on commercial activity in the city. The association of cause and effect in centre development and retail change is notoriously difficult. The attempts by Bennison and Davies (1980) to explore the effect of the Eldon Square Centre in Newcastle upon Tyne represent the best attempts yet but even in this case the attribution of commercial change due to centre development posed severe difficulties. Table 6.3 shows the framework in which impact studies may be placed. Three general spheres of impact are isolated, economic, environmental and social. Within each of these are a number of aspects of commercial activity which may be affected by the development. In some cases sound measurement techniques are available to determine the amount of commercial change, in other cases assessment is very subjective and may be heavily influenced by the analyst's own social and political values. Many of the impacts involve an assessment of the value of modernity or traditionalism within the provision of retail facilities. The awareness of the contrast between the new types of trading in the new shopping environment created by a shopping centre and the traditional retail provision of the surrounding shopping is highlighted in many studies of both consumer and retailer attitudes to renewal centre development.

In general, impact studies of shopping centres, particularly in respect of the consumer, are marginal to the central aim of this book. The purpose here is to consider the development process rather than to review the effects of developed centres. Impact studies are important, however, because they generate a feedback loop within the development process. Assessments of impact influence the attitudes of land use planners and centre developers towards future schemes. This is particularly important where a wide view of the impact is taken, as shown in Table 6.3, with land use planners adapting policy and its implementation in the light of the studies. When renewal centres form part of a comprehensive plan for a city centre, land use planners need to know what the likely effects of the centre will be in order to formulate other aspects of the plan. Now local authorities are actively involved again in centre development in Britain there is need for accurate forecasts of centre effect which relate to the social as well as to the economic health of the city.

The two examples considered in this chapter illustrate contrasting approaches to public control of centre development. Within France specific legislation has been created to slow the speed of development of focused centres. Within Britain control of renewal centres has been carried out both by using the general land use planning legislation and by public bodies becoming partners in development schemes. In both countries and with both centre types, government has been involved to protect society from an increase in the inequities of retail provision. In many cases assumptions have been made that developers lack social responsibility and so need to be controlled. Often such an assumption is quite unfounded although the few cases where it has had a basis in truth have been widely publicized. The evolution of both focused centre development in France and renewal centre development in Britain shows that as the shopping centre industry has matured so developers have responded increasingly to the social demands of both retailers and consumers. The curmudgeon argues this has taken place because of public policy intervention, the altruist suggests that social responsibility would have emerged without prompting from the policy makers.

Table 6.3 A framework for the study of the impact of renewal centres

ECONOMIC IMPACT		ENVIRONMENTAL IMPACT		SOCIAL IMPACT	
Positive	Negative	Positive	Negative	Positive	Negative
Adds new stock	Reduces old stock	Modernizes outworn areas	Changes traditional character	Allows for efficient shopping	May favour car-borne shoppers
Accommodates larger modern stores	Discriminates against small independents	Reduces land use conflicts	Creates new points of congestion	Provides new shopping opportunities	May limit choice to stereotypes
Increases rates and revenues	Increases monopoly powers	Scope for new design standards	Intrusive effects on older townscapes	Provides more safety	Creates new stress factors from crowds
Creates new employment	Changes structure of employment	Provides weather protection	Creates artificial atmosphere	Provides more comfort and amenities	Attracts delinquents and vandals
Improves trade on adjacent streets	Reduces trade on peripheral streets	Leads to upgrading of some streets	Causes blight on other streets	Concentrates shopping in one area	Breaks up old shopping linkages
Enhances status of central area	Affects status of surrounding centres	Integrates new transport	Causes pressure on existing infrastructures	Potentially greater social interaction	Becomes dead area at night

Source: After Bennison and Davies (1980)

CHAPTER 7
SHOPPING CENTRES IN THE FUTURE

Over the past half-century the shopping-centre industry has grown to be a significant contributor to urban growth. The concept of a planned and controlled operating environment for retailers has become widely accepted, explicitly by the retailers themselves and implicitly by the majority of consumers, who find shopping at shopping centres to their liking. Retailers have found such locations advantageous. They are saved expense in store construction, they benefit from locations in association with other retailers in the centre, the centre provides a ready-made identity and image into which the retailer can fit, and frequently a variety of support services is provided. These all have to be paid for in the rents retailers pay and the ability of centre developers to obtain relatively high rents depends on their ability to provide the full range of benefits. The benefits in turn allow retailers to generate greater sales volumes than would be possible in other locations. Consumer acceptance of shopping centres comes from recognizing the benefits of having a concentration of retail functions within which there is control over the degree of competition so that the variety of retail functions is managed and maintained. There can also be benefits from shopping within a physical environment which is purpose-designed for the activity. The costs of these benefits include the loss of the traditional, familiar, often 'comfortable', shopping environments and, with large centres, there are perhaps also the social and environmental costs associated with the impact of large and complex building structures. The actual implementation of individual centre development or of specific systems of centres in a city may create particular extra personal and social costs to groups of consumers in the city. At a general level, nevertheless, there would appear to be notable social and commercial benefits associated with retail provision within a system of shopping centres. It seems likely that shopping centres will continue to be developed in the coming decades although perhaps not along the same lines nor with the same emphases as in the past twenty years.

The spread of the shopping centre concept, both as a field for property investment and as a land use planning philosophy, to rapidly urbanizing middle-income countries seems likely to gather pace. Here there will be a strong distinction between general-purpose shopping centres serving the mass population in the growing metropolitan areas and the specialist centres aimed at the relatively small groups of upper-income and at tourist consumers. A significant component of the multiplier effect of tourist development appears to be the retail sales generated from tourists as consumers. This is clearly apparent in holiday centres in the Caribbean and in cities such as Hong Kong where dual systems of shopping centres have developed alongside each other serving on the one hand the local population and on the other the tourists. The widespread acceptance of the need for strong urban planning policies within Third World societies will perhaps be the most potent force, however, in the general development of small, general-purpose shopping centres in the coming decades.

This more widespread application of urban planning activity signals a broader social change and the acceptance of an alternative philosophy of urban growth. A similar broad change in philosophy also underpins the more widespread acceptance of shopping centres in cities in the socialist economies of Eastern Europe and the USSR. Both an increased concern with the distributive aspects of the economic system as living standards rise and also a change in the political philosophy of urban provision in favour of concentrations of facilities have created conditions favourable for the acceptance of the shopping centre concept and it seems likely to be implemented widely in East European and Soviet cities in the next two decades.

Pointers exist to suggest some of the future trends within shopping centre development in other regions and countries where there are already established shopping centre industries.

1. There is an increase in the rate of development of centres in middle markets. (See Ch. 4)
2. There is a growing interest, in the USA, in locations within central shopping districts. (See Ch. 2, Ch. 3, Ch. 4 and Ch. 5)
3. There are trends towards the general acceptance of a wider range of centre types with centres designed to meet the demands of particular consumer segments. (See Ch. 2)
4. There are indications that government, often through the land use planning mechanism, is taking an increasingly active and more positive role in the centre development process. (See Ch. 4 and Ch. 5, Ch. 6)
5. The greater variety of centre types will result in greater variety in the financing arrangements for centre development. (See Ch. 3)
6. The development industry will continue to be dominated by relatively few large companies and these companies seem likely to become more multinational in their operation. (See Ch. 1 and Ch. 2)
7. The social role of centres will take on greater significance as centres, particularly larger ones, become increasingly considered as balanced community centres. (See Ch. 2)
8. Centre designs will change to take account of energy conservation and of the social functions added to centres. (See Ch. 2 and Ch. 3)

These eight trends are simple extrapolations of changes already under way and pointed to in earlier chapters. They suggest a continuance of current patterns of evolution for the next two decades.

The increased interest in investment in middle markets is a feature common to the developers of many centre types. Mention has already been made of this trend in earlier chapters. Not only does the trend imply a more widespread diffusion of centres, but it also results in a changed development process with smaller investments over a shorter period. Such developments also result in individual centres accounting for a relatively large share of a community's retail sales and there are implications here for the impact of these centres on existing retail structures. Although not large in absolute size, new centres in middle markets can become the major retail complex in a small city and have a consequential disastrous effect on established retail districts and the predominantly independent and local chain retailers in these traditional districts. Within middle-sized cities the shopping centre is the vehicle by which the organization, technique and environment of retailing are modernized.

The renewed interest in central city sites in American cities, particularly cities of the north-east industrial belt pointed to in several earlier chapters, results from a variety of causes including federal government initiatives, a reduction in the availability of suburban sites, and possibly from a social conscience toward the physical condition of central cities and the level of retail provision in the central city and inner suburbs. Although in some cities the pressure for redevelopment is channelled into rehabilitation and the creation of pedestrian malls, there is an increasing number of cities where the newer types of centres are being integrated into such rehabilitation schemes in established CBDs. Specialist centres, infill centres and ancillary centres, all seem likely to be built in increasing numbers at central area locations. Again, as with the developments in middle markets, these centres are often of modest size, with fewer problems of finance, and they may pose no more problems of land acquisition than do large free-standing centres in the growing suburbs where land has been obtained by speculators.

The third trend, the development of various forms of specialist centres, complements the growing interest in city centre locations. It comes about through retailers' merchandizing policies, which are increasingly segmenting consumer demand and behaviour. These policies underlie the great variety of themes in speciality centres ranging from antiques to sport. Furthermore, as the understanding of the motivational and psychological aspects of consumer behaviour improves, there becomes scope for more than one form of general-purpose shopping centre. Centres will be designed specifically to meet demands of the *economic* shopper, the *recreational* shopper, or the *pragmatic* shopper, and so on. It is partly to meet some of these contrasting consumer motivations that focused centres (such as those based on hypermarkets) and specialist centres (based for example on direct sales through factory outlets) continue to be developed. Over the next twenty years it seems likely that the range of foci and themes for such centres will expand.

Government involvement in the centre development process is increasing. The extent to which this intervention will be regulatory or advisory will depend greatly on the extent to which developers and retailers accept social responsibility for the projects in which they are involved. This responsibility concerns an awareness not only of the commercial impact of development but also the environmental impact and the ethics of the social engineering inherent in any large centre project. One approach to meeting these social responsibilities, and one favoured by land use planning agencies, is to require the developer to provide social facilities within what are essentially shopping centres. At the minimum this may only mean the provision of a public car park, within a renewal centre, but in other cases it may mean the integration of a library, a sports centre and other community and cultural facilities within the shopping centre complex. Furthermore, the developer may be expected to provide these facilities as a contribution to the community hosting the shopping centre. Spending on environmental management, such as landscaping and habitat conservation around centres, often has been forced on somewhat unwilling developers. To protect society from developers with a poorly developed social conscience public policy measures, either to control excessive centre development or to slow the development process, have been considered necessary in several countries.

The variety of centre types will result in differences in the development process amongst centres and those variations will be noticeable, particularly in the financing of centres. Being essentially conservative, the institutions providing the finance for traditional free-standing centres will take time to respond to the changing needs of developers for finance and in the intermediate period a considerable variety of funding mechanism will be evident. It seems likely, however that the larger development companies will be able more easily to obtain access to finance and so development will remain dominated by a relatively few large companies. But it also appears unlikely that single ownership of very large centres will be feasible in the future for as development costs increase so joint ventures between financial and developmental institutions will become commonplace.

Concern about energy costs in centre operation certainly will lead to changes in design to make shopping centres more energy efficient. Building design already is reflecting this growing consciousness. Additionally, the consolidation of social facilities with shopping centres reflects the broader issue of energy conservation and the attempt by land use planning agencies in Europe to reduce the frequency of consumer trips. Large multi-use centres, either in established shopping districts or as suburban activity nodes, provide destinations for multi-purpose trips and a network of such centres can result in an overall reduction in travel demand. Furthermore, transport efficiency can be obtained in the service delivery for such centres, for example in consolidated goods delivery to the retailers. A somewhat similar rationale can be seen in the development of focused centres where convenience goods are provided in a way which encourages weekly or even monthly shopping trips and the maintenance of a relatively large stock of goods in the home. Although trip length may be increased, trip frequency is reduced. There are also social changes underway which affect consumer behaviour. Amongst these an increase in the proportion of women in paid employment, life-cycle changes, more technology in the home, and so on, all reinforce the movement toward fewer shopping trips for convenience goods (Dawson, 1982). There will be a role for the large general-purpose shopping centre and for the small strip centre which provide for forgotten items and casual sales, but the function provided by the large neighbourhood centre and the community centre can be met by focused centres based on large mass-merchandising stores. It is possible that a blurring of the distinction between community and focused centres will occur as anchor tenants in community centres become larger causing changes in merchandizing policies, and also as the non-anchor element in focused centres increases slightly (see Ch. 6), so improving the financial return on the centre development.

The shopping centre has become such an established feature of contemporary society that the concept is likely to evolve as the broader transformation to post-industrial society takes place in Europe and America. The major forecasts of social structure to the end of the century, both in Europe (Hall 1977) and North America have little to say on the distribution industry in general and nothing on shopping centres, despite their pivotal position in the lifestyles of several hundred million consumers. Yet within the post-industrial society the shopping centre seems set to become the focus of the community. The large regional centres already have a sizeable group of users who visit simply for enjoyment and to observe the world. Within such centres café tables are provided in the mall and here business deals are struck and social relationships made as they are in the street cafés of continental Europe. The difference is that the surrounding environment in the centre is carefully and consciously managed, unlike its counterpart in the streets of Amsterdam or Marseille. The large centres generate considerable employment in a wide range of skills and this seems likely to continue into a society where there is widespread technology substitution for labour.

Technological change in distribution generally may well lead in the longer term to some form of tele-shopping and delivery system for convenience goods, but it still seems likely that there will be a role for the larger, comparison goods-orientated, multi-use centre whether in the suburbs or in a historic shopping district or in a middle market. The many problems inherent in tele-shopping will make its widespread acceptance slow and dependent on the organization of efficient and economic delivery services. Analysts of post-industrial society also suggest that there will be an increase in the value placed on individual social relationships as a reaction to the impersonality of industrial society. It is paradoxical that increased social interaction can occur in large multi-use shopping centres but the rationale for this is that such centres provide a sense of place for the community. The strength of these centres in new suburban areas lacking any community identity is a notable aspect of contemporary urban society. The creation of new successful centres in downtown areas also may reflect the loss of community suffered by inner city areas with new multi-use centres providing a social focus for inner city communities. Kowinski (1978) has argued cogently that the large centres provide the archetypal post-industrial social environment where all social needs are provided for in a totally managed framework. Americans, he points out, now spend more time in shopping centres than anywhere else other than at home and at workplaces. By the century's end, it seems quite possible that this pattern will have spread to Europe. Over the same period, shopping centres may well become the places where American society spends more active time than anywhere else.

APPENDIX
GLOSSARY

Anchor tenants. See *key tenants*.

Common area. The area within a shopping centre not designed for rental to tenants, including landscaped areas, pedestrian areas and service facilities.

Common area charges. Income collected from tenants for operating and maintaining the common areas in a centre. Such charges are usually calculated on a pro-rata rate either in respect of gross retail floorspace or sales volume.

Comparison goods. Articles which are long-term purchases usually bought at irregular intervals. Quality, price and style are important factors in selection. Sometimes termed shopping goods.

Component financing. Financing of individual items of a shopping centre development, such as an integrated energy system.

Construction finance. Short-term finance sought for construction and pre-opening costs.

Convenience goods. Articles which are purchased regularly and usually frequently.

Equity financing. The portion of the total cost of a centre provided by the owners.

Gross floor area. *Gross leasable area* plus *common area*.

Gross leasable area (GLA) The total floor area occupied by rent-paying tenants. It is the income-producing area of a centre and excludes common areas.

Gross retail floorspace. The floor area of a shop unit for which rent is paid. It includes sales space, storage and public areas within the shop unit.

Guaranteed rent. The minimum rent from a centre irrespective of the sales achieved by tenants.

Hypermarket. A retail unit of at least 2500 m² sales space selling a wide and low-price range of food and a general range of non-food products. The store is operated on self-service principles with a *scrambled merchandizing* policy. Adequate car parking is associated with the store.

Impulse goods. Articles not actively sought by shoppers but purchased on impulse.

Key tenants. Tenants which it is anticipated will prove to have the major customer-drawing power in a centre. They are often large, widely known and respected retail or service enterprises. Also known as anchor tenants.

Kiosks. Retail units with generally less than 15 m² gross retail floorspace and often free-standing.

Net retail sales space. The area of the shop unit to which the public has access in order to purchase goods.

On-site parking. Parking provided as integral to the shopping centre.

Parking index. The number of car parking spaces per standard unit of GLA, this is usually 1000 ft². A frequently used standard in the USA is 5.5.

Parking ratio. The ratios of the site areas given over to parking and building.

Percentage lease. The most common type involves a tenant agreeing to pay a specified minimum rent related to gross retail floorspace and additionally a rent increment related to audited sales volume. The percentage rate and minimum rents are calculated on the basis of ability to pay, kind of business, shopping centre location, merchandising policy, etc.

Percentage rent. Rent based on a given percentage of the retail sales of tenants.

Sale and leaseback. A finance arrangement whereby the finance institution owns the land (or sometimes the whole development) and leases it to the developer.

Scrambled merchandizing. Selling a wide variety of goods but with a limited assortment of several types of goods.

Shopping arcade. A relatively narrow pedestrian way in an enclosed centre. Arcade widths are usually 4.5–6 m.

Shopping centre. A group of architecturally unified commercial establishments built on a site which is planned, developed, owned, and managed as an operating unit related in its location, size and type of shops to the trade area that the unit serves.

Shopping goods. See *comparison goods.*

Shopping mall. The part of an enclosed centre given over to pedestrian use and onto which shops front. Mall widths are generally 10–15 m wide. The term is also used to denote a large enclosed shopping centre.

Tenant association. An association of tenants operating in a centre, developer representatives and centre management, which provides a communication channel between tenants and management.

Tenant mix. The balance of tenants selected to operate in a shopping centre.

Tenant policy. The policy of developers which determines the types (organizational form, product mix, retail: service balance, etc.) of tenant which will operate in a centre.

Total capital cost. The sum of capital costs for land and land improvements, buildings and equipment, and overhead and development costs before opening.

Total operating receipts. The total income received by the owner of the centre including money received from rent, common area charges, *common area* facilities such as vending machines etc.

Trade area. The geographic area from which is obtained the major portion of a centre's trade. It is often split into primary (accounting for 60 per cent to 70 per cent of trade), secondary (an additional 15 per cent to 20 per cent) and tertiary trade areas.

REFERENCES

Abdullah, B. T. (1971) 'Suburban shopping centres in Singapore', *Berita Peranchang* **2**(1), 8–16.

Alexander, L. A. (1975) *The downtown shopping center: a new concept*, Downtown Research and Development Center, New York.

American Society of Planning Officials (1955) *Neighbourhood business districts*, Planning Advisory Service Information Report, 77.

Amery, C. and **Cruikshank, D.** (1975) *The rape of Britain*, Paul Elek, London.

Antill, L. (1981) 'Changes in district centres', *Chartered Surveyor* **113**(7), 494–6.

Applebaum, W. (1932) *The secondary commercial centres of Cincinnati*, University of Cincinnati.

Applebaum, W. (1970) *Shopping center strategy: a case study of the planning, location and development of the Del Monte Center, Monterey, California*, International Council of Shopping Centers, New York.

Applebaum, W. and **Schapker, B. L.** (1956) 'A quarter century of change in Cincinnati,' *Cincinnati Enquirer*, Cincinnati.

Applebaum, W. and **Kaylin, S. O.** (1974) *Case studies in shopping center development and operation*, International Council of Shopping Centers, New York.

Architecture in Australia (1969) 'Shopping centres' (special issue), *Architecture in Australia* (Feb.).

Architectural Record (1979) 'Retail malls', *Architectural Record* **165**(2), 117–32.

Arkitektur (1967) 'Rodovre Copenhagen shopping centre', *Arkitektur* **5**, 174–85.

Baker, G. and **Funaro, B.** (1951) *Shopping centers*, Van Nostrand Reinhold, New York.

Beaujeu-Garnier, J. and **Bouveret-Gauer, M.** (1979) 'Retail planning in France', in R. L. Davies (ed.) *Retail planning in the European Community*, Teakfield, Farnborough, 99–112.

Bell, C. C. (1975) *Shopping center development guide*, National Association of Home Builders, Washington D.C.

Bennett, D. W. (1971) 'Land costs push regional centers up and out', *Appraisal Journal* **39**, 606–9.

Bennison, D. J. and **Davies, R. L.** (1980) 'The impact of town center shopping schemes in Britain: their impact on traditional retail environments', *Progress in Planning* **14**(1), 1–104.

Berry, B. J. L. (1959) 'A critique of contemporary planning for business centers', *Land Economics* **35**, 306–12.

Berry, B. J. L. (1967) *Geography of market centers and retail distribution*, Prentice Hall, Englewood Cliffs.

Bijlani, H. U. (1977) *Urban problems*, Indian Institute of Public Administration, New Delhi.

Birnkrant, M. (1970) 'Shopping center feasibility study: its methods and techniques,' *Journal of Property Management* **35**, 272–9.

Brubaker, C. W. (1975) 'Tomorrow's malls: multi-use and better looking', *Chain Store Age* **51**(9), 33–4.

Burns, W. (1959) *British shopping centres: new trends in layout and distribution*, Leonard Hill, London.

Business Week (1964) 'Germans park and buy', *Business Week* 15 Aug., 58–60.

Campbell, R. W. (1974) 'Stages of shopping center development in major Latin American metropolitan markets', *Land Economics* **50**(1), 66–7.

Cassady, J. Jr. and **Bowden, W. K.** (1944) 'Shifting retail trade within Los Angeles metropolitan market', *Journal of Marketing* **8**(4), 398–404.

Centre for Advanced Land Use Studies (1975) 'Rent assessment and tenant mix in planned shopping centres', *CALUS*, Reading.

Chapin, F. (1965) *Urban land use planning*, University of Illinois, Urbana.

Chase, V. D. (1979) 'Regional remodeling: sound marketing is key to success', *Shopping Center World* **7**(3), 30–5.

Cleary, M. (1981) 'Shopping centers: a leader's perspective', in G. Sternlieb and J. W. Hughes (eds) *Shopping centers: USA*, Center for Urban Policy Research, Rutgers University, N.J., 297–301.

Cohen, Y. S. (1972) *Diffusion of an innovation in an urban system*, University of Chicago, Department of Geography, Research Paper, 140.

Cooper, M. B. (1973) 'A theory of power in the shopping center development process and comments on the possible legal dynamics', *Alabama Retail Trade* **43**(12), 1–4.

Davies, R. L. and **Bennison, D. J.** (1979) *British town centre shopping schemes: a statistical digest*, Unit for Retail Planning Information, Report Ull, Reading.

Davies, R. L. and **Bennison, D. J.** (1980) *The legacy of town centre shopping schemes in Britain*, Summer School Paper F18, Planning and Transportation Research Co., London.

Dawson, J. A. (1981) 'Shopping centres in France', *Geography* **66**(2), 143–6.

Dawson, J. A. (1982) *Commercial distribution in Europe*, Croom Helm, London.

Day, R. E. (1964) 'Europe's first: Germany has a U.S. style shopping center', *International Commerce* **70** (9 Oct.), 6–9.

Dean, A. O. (1977) 'Adaptive use: economic and other advantages', *American Institute of Architects Journal* **65**, 26–40.

DeŠpres, S. (1970) 'A descriptive model of tenant mix and location for a super-regional shopping center: a case study of four super-regional centers in North Eastern Ohio', MA thesis, Kent State University, Ohio.

Deutsche Bauzeitung (1970) 'Scandinavian shopping', *Deutsche Bauzeitung* **104**(2), 114–20.

De Vito, M. J. (1980) 'Retailing plays a key role in downtown renaissance', *Journal of Housing* **37**, 197–200.

Dumbleton, R. H. (1974) 'Cardiff's centre plan', *Town and Country Planning* **42**, 119–24.

Dunham, T. (1981) 'CBL and associates: mastering the middle markets', *National Mall Monitor* **11**(1), 30–50.

The Economist (1966) 'Germany: shopping the American way', *The Economist* **219** (2 April), 34.

Emmet, B. and **Jeuck, J. J.** (1950) *Catalogues and counters*, University of Chicago Press.

Epstein, B. J. (1967) 'The trading function', in J. Gottmann and R. A. Harper (eds) *Metropolitan on the move: geographers look at urban sprawl*, Wiley, New York, 93–101.

Foster, J. R. 1967) 'The effect of shopping center financing on the opportunity for occupancy by independent retailers', *Southern Journal of Business* **2**, 25–37.

Frazier, J. (1974) 'The impact of a regional shopping center on commercial spatial dynamics', *Virginian Geographer* **9**(2), 16–19.

Freis, J. (1978) 'Government intervention in France: how has it affected development?', *Retail and Distribution Management* **6**(2), 41–5.

French, R. A. (1979) 'The individuality of the Soviet city', in R. A. French and F. E. I. Hamilton (eds) *The socialist city*, Wiley, Chichester, 73–104.

Fry, J. N. (1961) 'Impact of a shopping center: the Wellington Square experience', *Traffic Quarterly* **26**(2), 89–96.

Gamzon, M. (1979) 'Design development opportunities center on four retail retailing trends', *Architectural Record* **165**(2), 71–3.

Garner, B. J. (1966) *The internal structure of retail nucleations*, Northwestern University Studies in Geography, 12.

Gosling, D. and **Maitland, B. L.** (1976) *Design and planning of retail systems*, Architectual Press, London.

Graham, D. H. (1966) 'Shopping centres: financing, appraisal and amanagement', *Journal of Property Management* **31**, 114–19.

Green, A. S. (1978) 'Orchard Square: foreign megastructure with implications that hit home', *Shopping Center World* **7**(4), 101–102.

Gruen, V. (1962) 'The suburban shopping center and urban core area', *American Review* **6**(2), 38–53.

Gruen, V. (1973) *Centers for the urban environment: survival of the cities*, Van Nostrand Reinhold, New York.

Gruen, V. and Smith, L. P. (1960) *Shopping towns U.S.A.*, Van Nostrand Reinhold, New York.

Guthrie, P. R. (1980) 'Statistical survey reveals effect on sales of store location inside mall', *Shopping Center World* **9**(5), 125–32.

Guy, C. (1980) *Retail location and retail planning in Britain*, Gower, Farnborough.

Hall, J. M. (1980) 'Covent Garden newly marketed', *London Journal* **6**(2), 215–22.

Hall, P. (1977) *Europe 2000*, Duckworth, London.

Harrison, T. (1968) 'The advent of the super-regional shopping center', *Appraisal Journal* **36**, 91–7.

Heeter, D. (1969) 'Toward a more effective land-use guidance system: a summary and analysis of four major reports', American Society of Planning Officials, Chicago.

Heirich, W. C. (1979) 'The 10 most common problems in renovation', *Shopping Center World* **8**(5), 138–42, 212–14.

Hermand, H. (1975) 'Loi d'orientation: anacronique, inadaptée', *Libre Service Actualite* **548**, 103–107.

Hillier Parker May and Rowden (1981) *British shopping developments*, Hillier Parker May and Rowden, London.

Hornbeck, J. S. (ed.) (1962) *Stores and shopping centres*, McGraw-Hill, New York.

House and Home (1974) 'The speciality shopping center', *House and Home* **23**(8), 67–77.

Housing (1980) 'Neighbourhood shopping centers: where to put them, how to fill them up', *Housing* (Sept.), 38–47.

Hoyt, H. (1933) *One hundred years of land values in Chicago*, University of Chicago Press.

Hoyt, H. (1958) 'Classification and significant characteristics of shopping centres', *Appraisal Journal* **26**, 214–22.

Hoyte, C. (1975) 'Recycling: and the route to more productive buildings', *Architectural Record* **158**, 96–101.

Huff, D. L. (1962) 'Determination of intra-urban retail trade areas', Real Estate Research Program, University of California, Los Angeles.

Institut Français du Libre Service (1973) *Intégration des indépendants dans les centres commerciaux*, IFLS, Paris.

International Council of Shopping Centers (1975) *Enclosed mall shopping centers*, ICSC, New York.

Japan Architect (1970a) 'Shopping mall: Senri New Town', *Japan Architect* **45**, 40–4.

Japan Architect (1970b) 'The Tamagawa Takashimaya', *Japan Architect* **45**, 15–18.

Japan Architect (1971a) 'Suburban shopping center: Daiei Nakamozu shopper's plaza, *Japan Architect* **46**, 103–106.

Japan Architect (1971b) 'Taba Pearl building and Toba Habour Center', *Japan Architect* **46**, 71–80.

Japan Architect (1973) 'Toba Building and shopping center', *Japan Architect* **48**, 82–8.

Johnston, M. R. (1973) 'Perth metropolitan region retail shopping survey', M. R. Johnston, Perth.

Jones, C. S. (1969) *Regional shopping centres: their location, planning and design*, Business Books, London.

Jones Lang Wootton (1978) *Location as a factor affecting investment in shops*, London.

Kivell, P. T. and Shaw, G. (1980) 'The study of retail location', in J. A. Dawson (ed.) *Retail geography*, Croom Helm, London, 95–155.

Kober, C. (1977) 'Regrowth for existing shopping centers', *Urban Land* **36**(2), 3–11.

Kober, C. (1981) 'Decade has seen three generations of urban redevelopment design', *Shopping Center World* **10**(1), 100–106.

Koehler, C. T. (1973) 'A comparative study of three suburban malls: the influence of physical environment on pedestrian behavior', *Journal of Environmental Systems* **3**(3), 17–25.

Koltz, L. (1973) 'Modernizing yesterday's shopping center', *Journal of Property Management* **38**, 118–23.

Kowinski, W. S. (1978) 'The malling of America', *New Times* **10**(9), 30–55.

Lakshmanan, T. R. and Hansen, W. G. (1965) 'A retail market potential model', *Journal of the American Institute of Planners* **31**, 134–43.

Leibowits, P. D. (1981) 'The preliminary track record', in G. Sternlieb and J. W. Hughes (eds) *Shopping centers: U.S.A.* Center for Urban Policy Research, Rutgers University, N.J., 219–27.

Lewison, D M. and Showalter, M. J. (1977) 'A possible impact of the New Columbia mall on Columbia's existing shopping clusters', *Business and Economic Review* **23**(6), 2–8.

Libre Service Actualité (1978) 'Investir a quel prix?: **3** le cas des hypermarches', *Libre Service Actualité* **652**, 81–4.

Libre Service Actualité (1981) 'L' indépendant: victime du centre commercial?', *Libre Service Actualité* **793**, 29–32.

Liepmann, C. (1973) *Intégration des indépendants dans les centres commerciaux*, Institut Français du Libre Service, Paris.

Linacre, V. (1980) 'Town centre development', *Estates Gazette* **253**, 887–9.

Linge, G. J. R. (1975) *Canberra: site and city*, Australian National University Press, Canberra.

Lion, E. (1976) *Shopping centers: planning, development and administration*, Wiley, New York.

Lisle, P. O. (1981) 'Investment: turnover too often forgotten in reviews', *Estate Times Review of Retailing* (Jan.), 45.

Mallen, B. and Savitt, R. (1978) *A study of leasing practices and retail tenant selection and restriction in shopping centres in Canada*, Bureau of Competition Policy, Department of Consumer and Corporate Affairs, Ottawa.

Mandelker, D. R. (1962) 'Control of competition as a proper purpose in zoning', *Zoning Digest* **14**, 33–41.

Marler, D. (1971) 'Developer as a partner: Newcastle-upon-Tyne central area shopping redevelopment', *Town and Country Planning* **39**, 313–17.

Mason, J. B. and Moore, C. T. (1972) 'A note on interchange location practices by developers of major retail centers', *Land Economics* **46**, 184–7.

Mayer, H. M. (1942) 'Patterns and recent trends of Chicago's outlying business centers', *Journal of Land and Public Utility Economics* **18**, 4–16.

Mayor's Commission (1973) *In city shopping centers*, Mayor's Commission, Chicago.

McCahill, E. (1976) 'Downtowns welcome back small shopping centers', *Planning* **420**(5), 15–17.

McGregor, C. H. (1960) 'Shopping centers', Small Business Administration, Washington DC, *Bulletin* **27**.

McKeever, J. R. (1973) 'Shopping center zoning', Urban Land Institute, *Technical Bulletin* **69**.

Merrenne-Schoumaker, B. (1976) 'Evolution recente des grands centres commerciaux en Belgique 1974–5, *Bulletin*, Société Geographique de Liège **12**, 51–63.

Ministry of Housing and Local Government *(1962) 'Town centres: approach to renewal'*, *Planning Bulletin* **1**, HMSO, London.

Ministry of Housing and Local Government (1963a) 'Town centres: cost and control of redevelopment', *Planning Bulletin* **3**, HMSO, London.

Ministry of Housing and Local Government (1963b) 'Town centres: current practice', *Planning Bulletin* **4**, HMSO, London.

Muller, P. O. (1981) *Contemporary suburban America*, Prentice Hall, Englewood Cliffs.

Muller, P. O., Meyer, K. C. and Cybriwsky, R. A. (1976) 'Metropolitan Philadelphia: a study of conflicts and social cleavages', in J. S. Adams (ed.) *Contemporary metropolitan America*, vol. 1, Ballinger, Cambridge, 217–90.

Muller, T. (1978) *The fiscal impact of regional malls on central business districts in small cities*, Urban Institute, Washington DC.

National Capital Development Commission (1981) *Retailing in Canberra*, Author, Canberra.

National Mall Monitor (1981) 'Speciality centres face tests of time', *National Mall Monitor* **11**(3), 40, 42, 176.

Northen, R. I. and Haskoll, M. (1977) *Shopping centres: a developer's guide to planning and design*, Centre for Advanced Land Use Studies, Reading.

Ognjenovic, D. (1980) 'North London's shopping city', *Retail and Distribution Management* **8**(4), 40–3.

Opsata, M. (1979) 'Developers recognize value and profit in center peripheral land', *Shopping Center World* **8**(7), 38–41.

Opsata, M. (1980) 'Good things come in small packages', *Shopping Center World* **9**(4), 28–32.

Opsata, M. (1981) 'Retail properties slip to second place as foreign investors pursue offices', *Shopping Center World* **10**(2), 27–30.

Pass, D. (1973) *Vallingby and Färsta: from idea to reality*, MIT Press, Cambridge.

Perenyi, I. (1973) *Town centres: planning and renewal*, Akademiai Kiado, Budapest.

Peterson, E. (1976) 'Trend to smaller centers: they're less complicated, cheaper, faster to build', *Shopping Center World* **5**(3).

Potter, H. and Dowling, R. W. (1943) 'Neighbourhood shopping centers', *Architectural Forum* **79**, 76–8.

Progressive Grocer (1965) 'Early American theme livens shopping center', *Progressive Grocer* **44**(8), 144–9.

Proudfoot, M. J. (1937) 'The outlying business centres of Chicago', *Journal of Land and Public Utilities* **13**, 57–70.

Qualite, P. (1974) 'Future hypers will form the hub of small towns', *Grocer* (30 Mar.), 58.

Real Estate Analyst (1970) 'Shopping centers still gaining on the central business districts', *Real Estate Analyst 39* (14 Aug.), 341–56.

Redstone, L. G. (1973) *New dimensions in shopping centers and stores*, McGraw-Hill, New York.

Redstone, L. G. (1976) *The new downtowns*, McGraw-Hill, New York.

Reinsdorf, J. (1981) 'Small shopping centers gaining investor attention', *Shopping Center World* **10**(3), 18–19.

Roberts, D. D. (1973) 'Management of shopping centres in the United States of America', *The Valuer* (Oct.), 624–32.

Roca, R. A. (ed.) (1980) *Market research for shopping centers*, International Council of Shopping Centres, New York.

Rouse, J. W. (1963) 'The regional shopping center: its role in the community it serves', *Ekistics* **16**, 96–100.

Sabit, J. and Black, H. (1962) 'The central business district', *Appraisal Journal* **30**, 69–74.

Sales Management (1970) 'Shopping centers USA: downtown in the cornfields', *Sales Management* **105**(11), 34–6.

Scarlat, A. (1963) *The development of shopping centres in the Stockholm area*, The Swedish Institute, Stockholm.

Schiller, R. and Lambert, S. (1977) 'The quantity of major shopping development in Britain since 1965, *Estates Gazette* **242**, 359–63.

Schmertz, M. F. (1974) 'New directions for downtown and suburban shopping centers', *Architectural Record* **155**, 137–52.

Schwartz-Barker, L. (1979) 'The changing strip: renewed interest in a forgotten stepchild', *Shopping Center World* **8**(1), 47–50.

Scott, K. and Gammie R. A. (1979) 'Specialty centres', *Estates Gazette* **251**, 353–5.

Seelig, J. H., Goldberg, M. and Harwood, P. (1980) 'Land use control legislation in the United States: a survey and synthesis', Economic Council of Canada, *Working Paper* **9**.

Shaw, G. (1978) 'Retail developments and structural change in West Germany', *Retail and Planning Associates* Corbridge.

Shinehouse, A. F. (1962) 'Financing shopping centres', *Banking* **55**, 52–3.

Shopping Center World (1973) Census of the shopping center industry *Shopping Center World*, **1**(12), 26–64.

Shopping Center World (1978a) 'The Arcade', *Shopping Center World* **7**(4), 124, 162.

Shopping Center World (1978b) 'The viability of downtown shopping centers', *Shopping Center World* **7**(2), 33–4.

Shopping Center World (1980a) 'Outlet malls gaining developers' interest', *Shopping Center World* **9**(5), 242–3.

Shopping Center World (1980b) 'South American Center utilizes several unique concepts', *Shopping Center World* **9**(8), 36–7.

Shopping Center World (1980c) 'The industry and mid-markets: one person's mid-market may be another's regional', *Shopping Center World* **9**(1), 60–72.

Shopping Center World (1981a) 'Multi-use development in "now concept"', *Shopping Center World* **10**(5), 148.

Shopping Center World (1981b) 'Not many options open if developers won't give up part of center deals', *Shopping Center World* **10**(7), 14–16.

Shopping Center World (1981c) 'Biennial census of reshopping center industry', *Shopping Center World*, **10**(1), 65–80.

Smith, B. S. (1977) 'Central area development: the German style', *Town and Country Planning* **45**, 362–5.

Smith, L. (1959) 'Analysis of the earning capacity of a shopping center', *Appraisal Journal* **27**(3), 305–20.

Smith, P. E. and Kelley, E. J. (1960) 'Competing retail systems: the shopping center and the C.B.D.', *Journal of Retailing* **36**(1), 11–18.

Solomon, N. (1981) 'Leasing problems: developers in growing chains', *Shopping Center World* **10**(1), 90.

Spalding, L. A. (1981) 'Shopping center futures', *Stores* **63**(10), 59–64.

Spiegel, E. (1966) *New towns in Israel*, Karl Kramer, Stuttgart.

Spink, F. H. (1981) 'Downtown malls: prospects, design, constraints', in G. Sternlieb and J. W. Hughes (eds) *Shopping centres*: U.S.A. Centre for Urban Policy Research, Rutgers University, N.J.

Spring, M. (1976) 'Self-service developers', *Building* **236** (1 June), 52–6.

Stambaugh, D. (1978) 'Proper tenant mix: how to put it all together', *Shopping Center World* **7**(4), 42–6.

Stenning, R. (1980) 'Covent Garden: alive and well', *Estates Gazette* **254**, 1077–83.

Stilwell, F. J. B. (1968) 'Location of industry and business efficiency', *Business Ratios* **2**, 5–15.

Strong, A. L. (1971) *Planned urban environments*, Johns Hopkins University Press, Baltimore.

Sweet, M. L. (1959) 'Tenant selection policies of regional shopping centers', *Journal of Marketing* **23**, 399–404.

Tarlock, A. D. (1970) 'Not in accordance with a comprehensive plan: a case study of a regional shopping center location conflict in Lexington, Kentucky', *Urban Law Annual*, 133–83.

Thil, E. (1966) *Les inventeurs du commerce moderne*, Arthaud, Paris.

Thorsen, W. L. (1974) 'Mini malls', *Urban Land* **33**(10), 11–18.

Unit for Retail Planning Information (1977) *District shopping centres*, UPRI, Reading.

Urban Land Institute (1975) *Dollars and cents of shopping centre*, 1975 Urban Land Institute, Washington DC.

Urban Land Institute (1966) *Dollars and cents of shopping centers* 1966 Urban Land Institute, Washington DC.

Urban Land Institute (1972) *Dollars and cents of shopping centers* 1972, Urban Land Institute, Washington DC.

Urban Land Institute (1978) *Dollars and cents of shopping centers* 1978, Urban Land Institute, Washington DC.

Urban Land Institute (1981) *Dollars and cents of shopping centers* 1981, Urban Land Institute, Washington DC.

Urban Land Institute (1977) *Shopping center development handbook*, Urban Land Institute, Washington DC.

Urban Land Institute (1980) *Downtown development handbook*, Urban Land Institute, Washington DC.

Vance, J. E. (1976) 'The American city: workshop for a national culture', in J. S. Adams (ed.) *Contemporary metrolitan America*, vol. 1, Ballinger, Cambridge, 1–49.

Villaneuva, M. (1945) *Planning neighbourhood shopping centers*, National Committee and Housing, New York.

Wacher, T. and Flint, A. (1980) 'How Covent Garden became a speciality shopping centre', *Chartered Surveyor* **112**(12), 594–600.

Wade, B. (1979) 'Retail planning in Britain', in R. L., Davies (ed.) *Retail planning in the European Community*, Saxon House, Farnborough, 51–63.

Walker, M. (1957) 'The impact of outlying shopping centers on C.B.D.'s', *Public Management* **89**(8), 170–4.

J. Walter Thompson Company (1954) *The shopping center in the United States*, JWT Co., New York.

Warner, S. (1981) 'Aging mall recaptures its lost youth', *Chain Store Age* **47**(3), 79–81.

Warren, J. (1973) 'Neighbourhood centre: a comparative study of neighbourhood centres in Sweden and Poland', *Royal Town Planning Institute Journal* **59**, 271–5.

Weijer, J. de (1975) 'The Karregat at Eindhoven (Holland)', *Build International* **8**, 239–57.

Welch, C. T. (1969) 'A guide to shopping centre planning', *National Building Research Institute Bulletin* **56**, Pretoria.

Westerman, A. (1966) *Swedish planning of town centres*, Swedish Institute, Stockholm.

Whitehall, W. M. (1977) 'Recycling Quincy Market', Boston', *Ekistics* **256**, 155–7.

Yeung, Y. M. and, **Yeh, S. H. K.** (1971) 'Commercial patterns in Singapore's public housing estates', *Journal of Tropical Geography* **33**, 73–86.

Yoshino, M. Y. (1971) *The Japanese marketing system*, MIT Press, Cambridge.

BIBLIOGRAPHY

There are several general bibliographies on shopping centres which have been published over the last 25 years. The major ones are:

Balachandran, M. (1976) *Malls and shopping centers: a selected bibliography (1970–75)*, Council of Planning Librarians, Exchange Bibliography, 1123, Chicago.

Dawson, J. A. (1982) *Shopping centers*, Council of Planning Librarians, Bibliography 89, Chicago.

Holmes, J. D. L. (1957) *Selected and annotated bibliography of the planned suburban shopping center*. University of Texas, Austin, Bureau of Business Research.

Kessler, M. A. (1971) *Shopping centers*, Council of Planning Librarians, Exchange Bibliography, 208, Chicago.

Kroger Company (1957) *Selected annotated bibliography of the planned suburban shopping center*, Kroger Company, New York.

Myers, R. H. (1970) *Suburban shopping centers*, United States Small Business Administration, Washington DC.

More specialist bibliographies are:

Duensing, E. (1980) *Suburban shopping centers vs. the central business district: a bibliography*, Vance Bibliography, P417, Monticello.

Gray, C. J. (1977) *Adaptive re-use: shopping malls from older buildings*, Council of Planning Librarians, Exchange Bibliography, 1314, Chicago.

Lalonde, B. J. and Smith, P. E. (1968) *A selected and annotated bibliography on shopping center management*, Michigan State University, East Lansing.

Regular censuses of shopping centre numbers in North America are presented in *Shopping Center World* and in France in *Libre Service Actualité*. In Britain, Hillier Parker May and Rowden and the Unit for Retail Planning Information provide lists of centres. Generally government statistics on shopping centres are poor or non-existent. Reports of new openings and trends in the industry are provided in *National Mall Monitor* and *Chain Store Age* for North America whilst in Britain *Retail and Distribution Management* reviews trends whilst new items are carried in *Shop Property, Estates Times* and *Estates Gazette*. Detailed case studies of the development of specific centres are provided in the Project Reference File of the Urban Land Institute.

INDEX